Principles of Operating Systems

2020 Edition

By Darrell Hajek, Cesar Herrera and Flor Narciso

Darrell Hajek received his PhD. In mathematics in 1971 from the University of Florida. He was immediately hired by the University of Puerto Rico at Mayaguez (RUM) and has been working there ever since, teaching mathematics and computer science (10 years as department chair.) He has approximately 50 mathematics publications in refereed journals as well as several books in computer graphics, computer literacy and fiction/fantasy.

Cesar Herrera worked in industry for several years. He received his MS in computer science from Ohio State University in 1985 and was hired by the University of Puerto Rico at Mayaguez (RUM). He served as an advisor in the development of the undergraduate computer science program in the Department of Mathematical Sciences, and as coordinator of the undergraduate computer science program for several years. Recently retired, he was a full professor at RUM. He has several publications in software engineering and human-computer interaction and was the primary teacher of operating systems in the Department of Mathematical Sciences for approximately 15 years. He is currently working as a consultant to academic institutions, providing expertise in the areas of databases and human computer interaction.

Flor Narciso received her MS in Informatics in 1988 from the Universidad Politécnica de Madrid, and her Ph.D. in Computer Science and Engineering in 1999 from the University of South Florida. She was a professor at the University of the Andes in Venezuela for 31 years, and in 2014 was hired by the University of Puerto Rico at Mayaguez (RUM), where she has been teaching computer science. She has participated in congresses, conferences and colloquiums, and has publications in congresses, conferences, scientific journals and chapters in books. Currently, she is the Acting Associate Director of the Department of Mathematical Sciences of the RUM.

Other books by Hajek and Herrera

Introduction to Computers

Introduction to Computers 2018 Edition

Introduction to Computers 2019 Edition

Introduction to Computers 2020 Edition

Principles of Operating Systems

Principles of Operating Systems 2019 Edition

Other books by Darrell Hajek

Introduction to Computer Graphics

Introduction to Computer Graphics 2018 Edition

Introduction to Computer Graphics 2019 Edition

Introduction to Office Productivity Software: Word-Excel-PowerPoint

IntroductionToOfficeSoftware:-Word–Excel–PowerPoint–Paint

Introduction to LibreOffice Productivity Software: Writer-Calc-Impress

Life and Times of Harry Wolf

Life and Times of Harry Wolf Expanded Edition

Life and Times of Harry Wolf Augmented Expanded Edition

Life and Times of Harry Wolf 2018 Edition

Life and Times of Harry Wolf 2019 Edition

Winning at Lotto

Preface:

We have noticed that very few students in our operating systems course were purchasing the assigned text. We quickly learned that they found it too expensive. Several (it is rumored) had resorted to downloading (illegal) electronic versions.

Not wanting to motivate illegal activities on the part of our students, we have set out to produce a more reasonably priced alternative.

We have tried to include all the material necessary for a basic course in operating systems, but, in order to keep a low price for our students, we have attempted to keep the content to ONLY what would be necessary for such a course. We fully expect that many will disagree with the choices we have made, both in what we have included and (probably even more) in what we have failed to include. We will revisit these decisions when we prepare future editions. Suggestions and recommendations are welcome.

We will be creating a set of supplementary PowerPoint files for the text as well as a testbank. We will be happy to make both available to any teacher who chooses to adopt the book as assigned text for a course.

You are welcome to contact us at:

darrell.hajek@upr.edu

or cesar.herrera@upr.edu .

or flor.narciso@upr.edu

Contents

1. Introduction

A *computer system* consists of several hardware components

processor, memory, system busses, storage devices (hard disk, optical drive, …), input devices (keyboard, mouse, …), output devices (monitor, printer, …)

as well as a LOT of software.

The software can be considered as being divided into two classes: operating system software and application software.

The operating system is an extremely important part of any computer system. An operating system has several functions. These functions include:

controlling access to the processor(s)

providing a set of services to users of the system

(providing the users with a means to interact with the system)

managing the system's hardware components.

1.0 Computing Systems

The primary function of any computing system is to process data.

1.0.1 The *Hardware* Components of a Computing System

The *hardware* components of a computing system generally include:

processing unit(s), memory, input device(s), output device(s), external storage, communications device(s), system buses.

1.0.1.1 **Processing Unit(s)**

A processing unit (also referred to as a CPU) controls the operation of the computer and performs the data processing functions. It executes the commands that result in the processing of the system's data.

1.0.1.2 **Memory**

Computer memory is often referred to using various names:

main memory, primary storage, memory, primary memory, random access memory, RAM.

RAM is "volatile", which means it loses its contents when the computer is shut down

Both the data being processed and the codes for the commands that control the actions of the CPU are stored in RAM.

1.0.1.3 **Input Device(s)**

A computing system requires devices that allow the user(s) to interact with the system, to enter data into the system's memory as well as to indicate activities that the user might want the system to perform.

1

The most common input device is the keyboard (for text entry) but pointing devices such as the mouse and trackball are also widely used.

1.0.1.4 **Output Device(s)**

A computing system must also have devices that communicate the processed information *to* users.

Devices such as monitors and printers.

1.0.1.5 **External Storage Devices**

Computing systems will typically need to store data and information for future use/reference. Because primary memory is (usually) volatile, systems will need devices that provide secondary storage. Devices where data and information can be stored for future use/reference.

Hard drives (magnetic storage), optical drives (CD, DVD), solid state drives (SSD)

1.0.1.6 **Communications Device(s)**

Devices that transfer data to and from other computing systems.

Devices such as modems and routers.

1.0.1.7 **System Buses**

Electrical connectors which allow the movement of data from one place to another among the components of a computer.

1.0.2 Operating System

An operating system has several functions;

It uses the system's resources, and controls access to them.

It provides a set of services for system users and manages secondary memory and I/O devices.

It controls the operation of the computer and performs necessary data processing functions.

1.0.2.1 Operating Systems tend to be quite Complex.

They are generally implemented as separate modules that can be evaluated and updated independently.

Among these are the *I/O modules* which control of movement of data between the computer and external environments.

These external environments include storage devices and communications equipment, as well as other I/O devices.

An operating system must coordinate communication with many different kinds of equipment and software and these units will have many different communication requirements. Over the years, a system has been developed in which operating systems provide standardized communication subprograms and the hardware and software developers create separate programs (called *drivers*, or in the case of communication with peripheral devices, *device drivers*) to interface their specific hardware or software with the standardized OS communication subprograms.

1.0.3 How the Computing System Works (Simplified)

The system memory (RAM) is divided into a number of *cells*, each of which has a numerical *address*. In some of the cells there will be codes for instructions that, when executed by the CPU, will cause the computer to process some data in the way that some user wants it processed.

The CPU has a register called the program counter, or PC. The PC will normally contain the address of one of the cells in memory.

The computer system continually repeats four operations. These operations are the following:

1. The contents of the cell whose address is in the PC are transferred (copied) into the CPU (data transfer by means of the system buses)
2. The contents of the PC register are incremented so that it no longer has the address of the same memory cell.
3. The uploaded data is interpreted as the code for a CPU instruction.
4. The CPU executes that instruction.

1.1 Operating Systems

Most readers will be at least somewhat familiar with the term "operating system". It is likely that they will have made use of more than one, and, if pressed, most could probably name some operating systems (UNIX, Linux, Windows, Android, IOS, ...)

However many (I suspect most) readers would have difficulty in describing just *what* an operating system IS.

An *Operating System* is a collection of programs, that manages the resources of a computer system, and provides interfaces between users, peripheral devices, system hardware and software.

Operating Systems are among the most complex pieces of software ever developed

1.1.1 Interfaces

An operating system would include (sub) programs that provide interfaces for:

- users and hardware;
- users and software;
- software and hardware;
- software and other software.

1.1.2 Services

Among the services offered by an operating system will be:

- Aids in program development (editors, debuggers)
- Program execution (loading program into memory and initiating execution)
- Access to I/O devices (hidden procedure to users),
- Controlled access to files (information protection),
- System access (resource protection- user identification and authorization),
- Error detection and response (division by zero, attempt to access forbidden memory location),
- Accounting (statistics for various resources).

An operating system will perform tasks like transferring data between main memory and secondary storage and like rendering output onto a display device.

1.1.3 Evolution

In our modern world, new kinds of hardware and software are continually being created, and any computing system is likely to incorporate some of these at various times in its lifetime. The operating system, then, must be capable of evolving over time in order to deal with changing system environments.

1.2 A Short History of Operating System Development

1.2.1 The Earliest Computers

(These were not really what we would call computers, today. By modern standards, they were little more than huge calculating devices.) They were "programmed" by setting combinations of switches and connecting wires between appropriate locations on circuit boards. When everything was set up correctly (at least the programmers *hoped* it was set up correctly) the main switch would be thrown and the "program" would start to execute. Output was often communicated by means of display lights on a console. There was nothing even remotely resembling what we would call an operating system. It would require a great deal of time just to set up a program to run. Users would access the computer one after another (in "series" so to speak.) Most installations used a simple sign-up sheet to reserve computer time, and of course, there were scheduling problems. Some of the programs would turn out to require more time than they had been allocated, and this would result in hard feelings (or worse.) Many programs would require less time than reserved. The system would then sit idle, waiting for the next user, who could not be counted on to come before his scheduled time. This would result in wasted computer time.

The system, as described above, was extremely slow (and error prone.) Computing systems were extremely expensive, and people who have invested lots of money to purchase a computer system generally like to get as much computing out of it as possible. Efficiency and speed were the primary motivating factors in most of the early computer development.

1.2.2 Von Neumann Architecture and Serial Batch Processing Systems

Probably the first really major step forward came when Jon Von Neumann proposed a system in which a computer program (as a sequence of binary codes for computer actions) might be stored in, and executed from, computer memory. Programs (and their data) could be read into computer memory (usually from punched cards or paper tape) and then could be executed from the codes stored in memory. This insight motivated the first primitive operating systems, which were developed in the mid-1950s. These were small *supervisor programs* (resident monitors) that provided basic I/O operations (such as control of punch card and/or tape readers and printers.) Not only can a machine read a deck of punched card a lot faster than a technician can figure out which sequence of switches to throw, but these systems allowed the system operators to submit sequences ("batches") of programs, to be read one after another. These systems were described as "batch processing systems." The system could read a program, execute it and immediately begin reading the next, without having to wait for the operator to load it.

1.2.2.1 Execution Modes

It was recognized almost immediately that user programs should not be allowed to read or write from the section of memory occupied and used by the resident monitor. Systems were designed to operate in different execution modes:

user mode (in which the programs were restricted to memory access with specific addresses and were not allowed to execute certain commands)

kernel mode (for the operating system only, in which the program would be less restricted as to its memory references and would be allowed to execute a wider range of commands.)

1.2.2.2 Operating System Overhead

The inclusion of an operating system clearly adds overhead to the system. Operating systems are programs and occupy space in memory. They take processor time to execute, but they are not, themselves, application programs. They are not programs submitted by users for execution but they do take up memory space and processing time that therefore will not be used by the user programs (the reason for having a computer system in the first place.) Nevertheless, even the simplest serial batch processing systems resulted in major improvements in efficiency and throughput of computing systems[1]. Loading a new pack of cards or mounting a new roll of tape requires a very long time (especially as computers experience time) but it does not take an operator much longer to load cards (or tape) for a sequence of four or five programs than it does to load just one.

---

[1] For one thing, the work of setting up (designing/writing) the program was all done offline, allowing the computer to execute other programs while this was going on. <The next sentence is a joke.> (An early example of "parallel" execution?) </That last sentence was a joke.>)

5

1.2.3 Several Programs in Memory at the Same Time

Then somebody figured out that very few programs actually use all the computer memory available, and that, as a consequence, it would usually be possible to fit the code (and data) for multiple programs into memory at the same time. If they did that, then usually, when one program finished, the system could immediately start executing another one. With the next program already in memory there would be no loss of time waiting for the program to load. The system would not have to wait for the cards or tape to start being read. Meanwhile, the operators could be loading the next set of cards or roll of tape while the original sequence of programs was running.[2]

Obviously, these systems required rather more sophisticated "*supervisor*" programs since they had more things to supervise. It would be necessary to keep track of where each program was located in memory, not only to know where to start the next program, but also in order to prevent an executing program from overwriting another waiting program (or the operating system itself.). In addition, the system would have to recognize when a program had finished, and, if there were more than one waiting program, it would have to select which would be executed next.

1.2.4 Multiprogramming

Early computer systems typically loaded all their data into memory, along with the programs, but, as computers began to be used for larger and larger collections of data, the amount of computer memory available in the systems began to put uncomfortable constraints on the amount of data that could be processed, and designers turned to external data storage (primarily tape) in order to deal with larger data sets. Of course, this meant that even more complex operating systems were required. They needed systems that could provide interfaces with these "new" kinds of external devices. It also meant that programmers were beginning to write programs that would attempt to access data stored on one of these external devices. When one of these programs would access one of these external devices (and it was starting to happen more and more frequently) the program would have to stop executing and wait for the data to be copied into memory where the program could make use of it. It was also becoming common for programs to store the results of their computations on external media. External input-output units were extremely slow (by computer execution standards) and these waiting periods were taking a (relatively) high toll on the system efficiency.

Given that many systems of the time were loading several programs into memory, the next step in operating system design was a system that would switch control to another program whenever an executing program had to stop and wait on an input/output device. In this way, the processor could be in more or less continual use, and this would result in greatly increased system efficiency. It would, of course, also require a much more complex operating system to accomplish this.

---

[2] Another example of the advantages of parallelism.

Naturally, when an I/O operation finishes, its associated program will have the data available that it needs to continue executing, and the operating system should identify the program as being ready to execute, so that when a running program stops, either finishing or requesting an I/O operation of its own, the original program can resume. All of this requires a system that can detect I/O operation completions, identify which of the paused programs were waiting on with these I/O operations, and return that program to the "waiting" list of programs ready to continue executing. It was to support these kinds of capabilities that *interrupt processing* was developed. It is interrupt processing that allows programs to return control to the OS when pausing to wait out an I/O operation (or when terminating.)

1.2.4.1 Processes

It was becoming common for programs to be designed having shorter relatively independent subdivisions.

This was especially true of operating systems. Operating systems, having become extremely complex systems, were being subdivided into subprograms.

For example, one subprogram might be used to submit requests for data from external media, another might transfer control to a "waiting" program, when an executing program has paused, and still another might place a "paused" program back into the waiting queue when its I/O operation has completed.

Operating systems were not the only complex programs/systems in the computer science universe, and the technique of dividing complex programs into smaller simpler subdivisions was becoming pervasive. It became common, then to speak of the OS as dealing with (and consisting of) *processes*, rather than *programs*.

A *process* can be defined as an entity that can be assigned to, and executed on, a *processor*. It is a unit of activity characterized by a single sequential thread[3] of execution, a current state, and an associated set of system resources.

A process contains three components: ***executable code***, ***the associated data*** needed by the process (variables, work space, buffers, etc.) and the ***execution context*** (or "process state") of the program. The execution context is essential because it is the internal data by which the OS is able to supervise and control the process. The execution context includes the contents of the various process registers, as well as other information such as the priority of the process and its state (waiting to execute or paused, if waiting on I/O, identification of the event, ...)

---

[3] A **thread** of execution is defined to be the smallest sequence of programmed instructions that can be managed independently by a **scheduler**. *Threads* differ from traditional *processes* in that:
- processes are typically independent, while a thread must exist as a subset of a process.
- processes carry considerably more state information than threads, whereas multiple threads within a process share process state as well as memory and other resources
- processes have separate address spaces, whereas threads share their address space
- processes interact only through system-provided inter-process communication mechanisms

1.2.5 Time Sharing

It was very quickly recognized that the system of loading several programs in memory at the same time and allowing another process to take over when an executing process has paused (i.e. *multiprogramming*) brought about a fundamental change in the way that the performance of computer systems should be *evaluated*. Previously, when an executing program had to finish before another could start, the emphasis was entirely on getting each program to execute as fast as possible[4]. Now, however, with systems in which several programs could be sharing access to the processor, the emphasis (at least in many installations) switched from how fast *one* program could be processed to how many programs could be finished in a given time period. At the same time, the price of memory (RAM) was coming down, which resulted in systems with capacities for greater numbers of simultaneous programs.

With this change of emphasis, came the realization that "compute bound" programs (programs that seldom stopped to wait for I/O) tended to block the progress of other programs in the system. Such programs would take control of the CPU for long periods of time without relinquishing it. I/O bound programs, on the other hand, would spend much of their time waiting for data transfer, and would use relatively little of the processor time. A computing system could support a larger number of I/O bound programs since, at any given time, many (probably most) of them would be in a suspended state and placing no load on the CPU.

In order to permit the I/O bound programs to proceed (once their blocking I/O operation had finished) it was found to be desirable to force the compute bound programs to relinquish control at regular intervals, and the system of "time slicing" was developed. When a process would begin executing, it would be assigned a "slice[5]" of time, during which it would be allowed to use the processor. If the process paused for an I/O operation, it would be placed in a "suspended" state, another waiting process would be awarded a time slice and allowed to proceed. When the I/O operation finished, the state of the suspended process would be changed to "waiting" and it would be placed in the list of processes waiting their turn for CPU time. In the event that a slice of time expired before the process paused for I/O (or for any other reason) the process would be interrupted, placed in a waiting state, the next process in the waiting list would be assigned a time slice and the interrupted process would be placed in the waiting list.

1.2.6 Interactive Multiuser Systems

It soon occurred to system designers (and purchasers) that it might be convenient to allow users to interact directly with the computer systems, rather than requiring them to physically hand over their programs (usually as packs of punched cards) to operators, and then wait for the programs to produce printed output that would then be handed back

---

[4] The related problem of choosing programs that would execute quickly was seen as more political (in the sense of *office politics*) than technical.

[5] Sometimes referred to as a "quantum"

(probably the following morning.) At this time, teletype terminals were becoming relatively common, and provided a convenient means for communication with computing systems. Such direct human interactions would tend to be quite I/O intensive since human response time is *much* slower than that of computers. Even a relatively large number of simultaneous "online" users would add relatively little to the cpu load, since an interactive program would spend much of its time in a paused state, waiting for a user to do something.

Interactive support systems were designed to allow users to write, compile, and execute their own programs online from computer terminals. This in turn helped to lower operational costs, since fewer personnel were needed to load programs and data (users were doing that themselves from their terminals.) It also opened computer access to a much wider group of people.

1.2.7   Systems with Virtual Memory

The growing number of multiuser interactive systems was creating situations with larger and larger numbers of programs sitting in a suspended state waiting for user input, and, at the same time, external storage systems (hard disks) were being developed with access times that, although terribly slow from the point of view of the CPU, were essentially instantaneous from the point of view of a human user. These external storage systems were (and are) much cheaper than RAM. It seemed obvious, then, that even larger numbers of users could be accommodated (on systems of the same price) if some of these suspended programs could be stored on disk until ready to resume execution, rather than occupying (relatively) expensive RAM.

Virtual memory systems were developed to transfer to disk contents of memory that were unlikely to be referenced in the immediate future. These might include programs that were paused waiting on I/O but could also include subsections of executing programs, if these sections did not involve code or data likely to be referenced soon.

Of course the management of these virtual memory systems required operating systems even more complex than earlier systems. These OS's now had to identify which programs and/or program segments would not be referenced immediately and keep track of where on disk the segments were stored. They needed the ability to retrieve these programs and/or segments and to locate space in RAM to copy them to upon retrieval. This had to be done in a way that the segments would be compatible with any other segments already in RAM and it had to be done relatively quickly (at least from the point of view of online users.)

Virtual memory can be an effective strategy for dividing large programs largely because of the *"Principle of Locality"*.

1.2.7.1 Principle of Locality

This principle states that memory references by the processor tend to cluster.

Most programs include sections of sequential code and these command codes will be close together (one after another) in memory. Programs frequently include *iterations* (sections of code that, once initiated, are executed multiple times.) Data is often stored as arrays, which are stored sequentially, and programs tend to reference multiple entries in a given array. In general, then, if a program references a given location in RAM, either for the code for an instruction or for data to process, it is likely that the next few memory references will be to locations close to that same location.

If, for a reasonable period of time, none of the cells in a particular section of memory have been referenced, then it is likely that the next several memory references will continue to be to cells in some different section of memory, and so, if the "not to be referenced" section were to be swapped out, the system performance would not be affected (at least for a while.)

Locality of reference for user software has recently weakened somewhat. This is mostly attributed to the spread of object-oriented programming and the increased use of sophisticated data structures like trees and hash tables. Object oriented programming tends to make use of large numbers of small functions. Structures like trees and hash tables tend to result in chaotic memory reference patterns.

1.2.8 Systems with Cache Memory

It did not take systems designers long to figure out that there could be benefits applying the principle of locality in the other direction as well.

If a CPU references a cell in a given section of RAM, then it is likely that the next few memory references will also be to cells in that same section.

New technology was being developed that permitted the creation of RAM that supported much faster memory references. Unfortunately, this newer faster RAM was also much more expensive, used more power and produced more heat. It was not (and still is not) cost effective to build computers in which the high speed technology was used for *all* of the RAM, but it *was* (and is) possible to include a relatively small amount of high speed RAM (called a cache.) When the processor references a location in normal RAM, the section of memory containing that cell can be copied into the cache, and, by the principle of locality, the next several memory references can probably be made to locations in high speed RAM in the cache, rather than regular RAM. In this way, although only a small amount of memory used high speed technology, most of the CPU operations *would* be executed using that memory. Of course, in systems with cache memory, the operating system has the additional responsibility of keeping track of which memory sections are duplicated in cache, which sections have been referenced recently, and which cache cells have had their contents modified (so new values have to be copied back to regular RAM before being replaced by more recently accessed memory sections.)

1.2.9 Systems with Disk Caches

Many programs do a great deal of disk I/O, frequently saving data to disk and/or retrieving data from disk. The progress of such programs is very much impeded by the relatively slow disk access times (as compared to CPU operations and RAM access.) Of course, the principle of locality also applies to disk access, so, in order to speed the progress of these I/O bound programs, systems similar to memory cache systems were designed that retain copies of recently referenced sections of disk in RAM where they could be referenced more quickly. In such systems, now the OS must track which sections of RAM are associated with which sections of disk, but also must deal with problems of data integrity, since it is possible that the system might shut down after a program has made changes to a virtual disk segment in RAM (which is, of course volatile) but before that modified segment has been copied to disk.

1.2.10 Personal Computers

The earliest computers were large and expensive, and, as time passed, computers became even larger, much more expensive and much much more complex. In the 1960's, however, segmentation of the computer market began to develop. Less complex and less expensive computers (minicomputers) entered the market. This division of the market did not, have an important effect on operating system development until the mid 1970's when the invention of the microprocessor made it possible for computer companies to begin marketing personal computers to individuals.

A [i]**microprocessor** is a computer processor that incorporates all the functions of a CPU on a single integrated circuit (IC). The integration of a whole CPU onto a single chip reduces the cost of processing power and increases efficiency. Integrated circuit processors are produced in large numbers by highly automated processes, resulting in a low per-unit cost. Single-chip processors increase reliability because there are many fewer electrical connections to fail.

Texas Instruments TMS1000.

Before the development of microprocessors, small computers had been built using racks of circuit boards with many medium- and small-scale integrated circuits. Microprocessors combined this into one large-scale IC.

Intel 4004.

Continued increases in microprocessor capacity have since rendered other forms of computers almost completely obsolete. Everything from the smallest embedded systems and handheld devices to the largest mainframes and supercomputers will use one or more microprocessors.

Before the introduction of the personal computer, all computer systems were operated by trained specialists, but, of course, this would not be the case with the personal computers. The advent of personal computers,

Motorola 6800.

11

then, made the user interface a much higher priority in operating system design. Obviously, systems that were easier to use (more "user friendly") could be marketed to a much wider audience. The earliest personal computer operating systems were running on systems with very limited resources (small amounts of RAM, external storage that was slow and had limited capacity, relatively slow processors.) The earliest personal computer operating systems tended to feature menu driven interfaces that were relatively simple to implement and required relatively few resources, as well as being easy for inexperienced users to understand and use.

Later, the personal computers became larger and faster, and started to come with bigger and faster external storage systems and larger displays. More complex interface systems known as Graphical User Interfaces (GUI's) were developed that made the personal computer even easier for untrained people to use.

1.2.11 [ii]Multiprocessors

In their never-ending search for ways to make computers work even faster, designers began creating *multiprocessors*, that is, chips which contain multiple processors[6], with the idea that several cores could process different processes simultaneously, and thus process data several times faster than could a single processor.

Of course effective use of a multiprocessor requires that some part of the system be capable of identifying which processes could be processed simultaneously and which were inherently sequential (one having to complete before the next could begin.)

Multiprocessor systems have a number of advantages over single processor systems. Principal among them, of course, is the capability of executing (at least some) programs faster, but, in addition, there is the factor that they are more robust. If one processor fails, the system can continue functioning (although probably at a somewhat reduced efficiency.)

Diagram of a generic dual-core processor with CPU-local level-1 caches and a shared, on-die level-2 cache.

Multiprocessor systems have the disadvantage of requiring a much more complex operating system (among other things, capable of identifying the processes that can be executed simultaneously and the need to identify and avoid deadlock situations.) These operating systems will require more memory and take more time to run than simpler purely sequential systems. Thus, for a purely sequential problem, a multiprocessor system would probably end up being slower than a system with only one processor (assuming that the single processor is as fast as any one of the multiple processors in the multiprocessor, of course.)

---

[6]   referred to as "cores" A **multi-core processor** is a single computing component with two or more independent processing units called cores, which read and execute program instructions

1.2.12 Smart Phones

With the arrival, and wide public acceptance of the smart phone (a combination of cell phone and computer) came a different set of priorities and constraints for operating systems.

Smart phones have relatively small displays

Most of their users have no formal training and limited experience in the use of computers.

There was also an obvious need for the operating system of a smart phone to provide an efficient interface with the telephone's communications system.

There are many more smart phones than any other kind of computer[7], and so the operating systems on smart phones constitute the vast majority of the operating systems currently extant.

1.2.13 Embedded Systems

Computing system hardware has become quite cheap and is now commonly built into other products (household appliances, automobiles, pacemakers, ...)

The embedded systems are designed for specific functions, and their operating systems are very different from the systems for general purpose computers, and, indeed, from one another. An embedded system's key feature is dedication to specific functions, but they often require strong general-purpose processors. For example, router and switch systems are embedded systems. Embedded routers function more efficiently than OS-based computers for routing functionalities.

Commercial embedded systems range from digital watches and MP3 players to giant routers and switches. Complexities vary from single processor chips to advanced units with multiple processing chips.

Of course embedded systems need operating systems in order to function. An **embedded operating system** is an operating system designed for an embedded computer system. There are many different kinds of embedded systems with many different functions, and so there are many different kinds of embedded operating systems, but most have a number of common characteristics. An embedded operating system is typically designed with high priorities on reliability and resource-efficiency. Resource efficiency comes at the cost of losing some of the functionality or granularity that larger computer operating systems provide. There will often be functions that would never be used by the specialized applications of the embedded system. Depending on the method used for multitasking, this type of OS is frequently considered to be a real-time operating system, or *RTOS*.

---

[7] General purpose computer, i.e. computer operated directly by a human user. There are probably many more *embedded* computers than smartphones.

The hardware running an embedded operating system can be very limited in resources (such as RAM and ROM) and therefore embedded design of these operating systems may have a narrow scope tailored to a specific application in order to achieve desired operation under these constraints. In order to take better advantage of the processing power of the CPU, software developers may write critical code directly in assembly language. This *machine efficient* language can (at least potentially) result in gains in speed and size, but usually at the cost of portability and maintainability. Many embedded operating systems, however, are written entirely in more portable languages, like C.

An important difference between most embedded operating systems and desktop operating systems is that the application, including the operating system, is usually statically linked together into a single executable image. Unlike a desktop operating system, the embedded operating system does not load and execute applications. This means that the system is only able to run a single application.

1.2.14   Network Operating Systems

As communication has become such a major factor in the utilization of computers, it has become essential for operating systems to deal with computer communication and networking.

The term **network operating system** is has come to be used with reference to two rather different kinds of systems:

- A specialized operating system for a network device such as a router or switch
- An operating system oriented toward computer networking. This kind of operating system is designed to support sharing things like files and printers among multiple computers in a network. Such an operating system enables the sharing of data, users, groups, security, applications, and other networking functions.
  - ✓ In fact, most modern operating systems include these kinds of features.

Early microcomputer operating systems such as CP/M, AppleDOS, MSDOS and classic Mac OS were designed for one user on one computer, but as local area network technology became available, systems were needed to use and deal with the technology. Two distinct approaches began to evolve for handling the kind of sharing required by networks: peer-to-peer and client-server.

1.2.14.1   Peer-to-peer (P2P) Networks

In a peer-to-peer network operating system users are allowed to share resources and files located on their computers and access shared resources from others. A peer to peer system does not have any centralized management source. All connected computers are equal, that is, they all share the same abilities to use the resources available on the network.

The advantages of a peer-to-peer network include:
- Ease of setup
- Less hardware needed,
  - ✓ no server need be acquired

The disadvantages include:
- No central location for storage
- Less security than the client–server model

1.2.14.2 Client-Server Networks

In a network operating system based on a client–server model, a *server* enables multiple *clients* to share resources.

Client-server network operating systems allow functions and applications to be centralized in one or more dedicated file servers. The server, then, is the *center* of the system, and allows client access to resources. The server can also provide security.

The network operating system provides the mechanism to integrate all the components on a network and allow multiple users to share the same resources (simultaneously) regardless of physical location.

The advantages of the client-server model include:

- Greater stability (centralized servers are more stable)
- Better security (security can be provided through the server)
- Greater flexibility (new technology and hardware can be easily integrated into the system)
- Better performance (hardware and the operating system can be specialized, with a focus on performance)
- Remote access (servers can be accessed remotely from different locations and types of systems)

The *dis*advantages of the client-server model include:

- Buying and running a server raises costs.
- Dependence on a central location for operation.
- Requires regular maintenance and updates.

1.2.15 System Implementation

The first operating systems were programmed in machine and assembly languages, however systems became more complex and it became clear that they would require frequent updates and modifications. The difficulty inherent in using such low level languages for working with such complex systems motivated efforts to create high level languages that could be used for systems development. Three of the better known systems development languages were BLISS (used by DEC), JOVIAL (used by USAF and its contractors) and PL/S (used by IBM.) By far, however, the best known example of an operating system programmed in a high level language is UNIX, which is famous for having been programmed in C.

There are a number of advantages to using a high level language for operating systems development. Code can be written faster, it is more compact and much easier to debug. In addition, high level language code is much more portable, since moving the system to a new platform requires little more than a compiler for the language on that platform.

1.3 Chapter 1 Exercises

1.3.1 "Virtual Reality Headsets" have become much more common recently. Does this type of output device pose any new types of problems or special requirements for operating systems?

1.3.2 What are the relative advantages and disadvantages of the various types of external storage devices?

1.3.3 Section 1.1 lists the names of 5 operating systems, all of which are currently in wide use (and this list is far from exhaustive, there are many more.) Why are there so many different kinds of operating systems? What are some advantages and disadvantages of some of the OS's in the list?

1.3.4 Explain the difference between multiprogramming and multiprocessing.

1.3.5 Explain the difference between Virtual memory and cache memory.

1.3.6 In P2P networks, unlike client-server systems, the content-serving capacity of the network can actually *increase* as more users begin to access the content. Explain how this can be.

1.4 Chapter 1 Questions:

1.4.1 True-False

1.4.1.1 The primary function of a computing system is to process data.

1.4.1.2 ROM is "volatile", which means it loses its contents when the computer is shut down.

1.4.1.3 Operating Systems are among the most complex pieces of software ever developed.

1.4.1.4 Portability and ease of use were the primary motivating factors in most of the early computer development.

1.4.1.5 On the earliest computers there was nothing even remotely resembling what we would call an operating system.

1.4.1.6 The development of sophisticated I/O device interfaces allowed programs to return control to the OS when pausing to wait out an I/O operation (or when terminating.)

1.4.1.7 "compute bound" programs (programs that seldom stop to wait for I/O) tend to block the progress of other programs in systems without time slicing.

1.4.1.8 "external storage systems were (and are) much cheaper than RAM.

1.4.1.9 The 1960's saw a segmentation of the computer market as less complex and less expensive computers (minicomputers) entered the market. This division of the market had an immediate impact on operating system development.

1.4.1.10 The advent of personal computers, made the user interface a much higher priority in operating system design.

1.4.1.11 With the arrival, and wide public acceptance of the smart phone (a combination of cell phone and computer) manufacturers were able to use simpler user interfaces since few of the phones were being used for complex programming tasks.

1.4.1.12 Embedded systems are designed for specific functions, and their operating systems are very different from the systems for general purpose computers, and, indeed, from one another.

1.4.1.13 An embedded system's key feature is dedication to specific functions, and for this reason they normally require specialized processors.

1.4.2 Multiple Choice

1.4.2.1 The operating system is an important part of the software of any computer system. An operating system has several functions. One of these functions would be:
a. controlling access to the processor(s)
b. providing a set of services to users of the system (determining how they can interact with the system)
c. managing system hardware components
d. all of the above
e. none of the above

1.4.2.3 The first primitive operating systems, which were developed in the mid-_____ were small supervisor programs that provided basic I/O operations (such as control of punch card and/or tape readers and printers.)
a. 1940s
b. 1950s
c. 1960s
d. 1970s
e. none of the above

1.4.2.4 Locality of reference for user software has recently weakened somewhat. This is mostly attributed to the spread of
a. object oriented programming
b. trees as data structures
c. hash tables
d. all of the above
e. none of the above

1.4.2.5 The 1960's saw a segmentation of the computer market as less complex and less expensive computers (_____) entered the market.
a. minicomputers
b personal computers
c. microcomputers
d smartphones
e. none of the above

1.4.2.6 The _____'s saw a segmentation of the computer market as less complex and less expensive computers (minicomputers) entered the market.
a. 1960
b   1970
c   1980
d   1990
e. none of the above

1.4.3 Completion

1.4.3.1 A processing unit (also referred to as a _____) controls the operation of the computer and performs the data processing functions. It executes the commands that result in the processing of the system's data.

1.4.3.2 Common input devices are keyboards and _____ devices such as trackballs or mice.

1.4.3.3 The operating system's I/O _____ provide control of movement of data between the computer and external environments, including: storage devices, communications equipment and other I/O devices.

1.4.3.4 An Operating System is a program, or collection of programs, that manages the _____ of a computer system.

1.4.3.5 The first primitive operating systems, which were developed in the mid-1950s were small *supervisor programs* that provided basic I/O operations (such as control of punch card and/or tape readers and printers.) The systems using these were described as _____ processing systems.

1.4.3.6 The inclusion of an operating system adds _____ to the system. Operating system programs occupy space in memory and they take time to execute, but are not, themselves, application programs.

1.4.3.7 A process contains three components: ***executable code, the associated data*** needed by the process and the ***execution*** _____ (or "process state") of the program.

1.4.3.8 _____ *memory* systems were developed to transfer to disk contents of memory that were unlikely to be referenced in the immediate future.

1.4.3.9 It was not cost effective to build computers in which the high speed technology was used for *all* of the RAM, but it *was* possible to include a relatively small amount of high speed RAM (called a (n) _____ .)

1.4.3.10 The earliest personal computer operating systems tended to feature _____ driven interfaces.

1.4.3.11 As personal computers became larger and faster, more complex interface systems (_____'s) were developed that made the personal computer easier for untrained people to use.

2. Characteristics of Operating Systems

As stated earlier, a computing system requires a set of resources for the processing, moving and storing of data. [iii]Common system resources include the central processing unit (CPU), computer memory, file storage, input/output (I/O) devices, and network connections. A computing system also requires a system of buses to move data from one resource to another. An operating system manages these resources and provides interfaces[8] for coordination among them.

Thus, the OS is responsible for managing and coordinating the system resources, and, in addition, must provide interfaces for communication between:

users,

software,

hardware,

and peripheral devices.

For the earliest operating systems, the main priority in design of computing systems was efficiency/speed of execution and this was interpreted as being how fast each single program could be processed.

When systems were developed which could load more than one program at a time, the emphasis shifted, and a higher priority was given to the number of programs that could be executed in a given time period, and a lower priority to the time for individual programs/jobs.

Then, as computers became bigger and faster, and were being used in a greater variety of situations, other factors began to take on greater importance, factors such as:

convenience
ease of use
portability
stability
security

---

[8] An **interface** is a shared boundary across which two or more separate components of a computer system exchange information.

Operating systems used on small devices *may* be relatively simple, but popular operating systems for these devices (Windows, OSX and Linux among them) also make use of *drivers* for a wide range of devices, as well as complex sophisticated user interfaces.

The core part of an operating system is its *kernel*.

The **kernel**[iv] is a computer program that is the core of a computer's operating system, with complete control over everything in the system. On most systems, it is one of the first programs loaded on start-up (after the bootloader). It handles the rest of start-up as well as input/output requests from software, translating them into data-processing instructions for the central processing unit. It handles memory and peripherals like keyboards, monitors, printers, and speakers.

Kernel Layout

One of the functions of a kernel is to provide an interconnection between application software and the computer hardware.

The critical code of the kernel is normally loaded into a separate area of memory, that is protected from access by application programs or other, less critical parts of the operating system. The kernel performs its tasks such as executing processes, managing hardware devices (hardware devices such as the hard disk) and handling interrupts, in this protected *kernel space*. In contrast, everything a *user* does (writing text in a text editor, running programs using a GUI, etc.) is done in *user space*. This separation prevents user data and kernel data from interfering with each other, causing instability and slowing the system down. It also keeps malfunctioning application programs from crashing the entire system.

Graphic of a monolithic kernel running kernel space entirely in supervisor mode

When a process makes requests of the kernel, the request is called a *system call*. Kernel designs differ in how they manage these system calls and resources. A *monolithic kernel*[v] runs all the operating system instructions in the same address space (resulting in better execution speed.) A *microkernel* runs most processes in user space, for modularity.

Today, monolithic kernels[9] are the most popular. These kernels provide a way for different computer processes to

Microkernel architecture relies on user-space server programs

---

[9]   A **monolithic kernel** is an operating system architecture in which the entire operating system is working in "kernel space" and is alone in supervisor mode. The monolithic model differs

send messages to each other, and they manage the RAM that stores program information. Most kernels also use device drivers to control monitors, input devices, disk drives and other peripherals.

2.1 Characteristics of the Execution of an Operating System Program

In the end, an operating system consists of software (i.e. programs) and these programs, just like any other programs, must be processed by a CPU. They are just sequences of instructions that must be executed.

There are, however, a few characteristics that are unique to operating system programs. For one thing, many operating system programs must have certain "*executive* privileges" that are not available to typical application programs. For another, many operating systems programs relinquish and regain control of the processor with much greater frequency than just about any other kind of program. Finally, efficiency and reliability are much more important in the design of an operating system than they are in the design of almost any other kind of program.

[vi]2.1.1 Some OS Programs have Executive Privileges

There are some activities that common application programs should never be allowed to perform and areas of memory that they should not be allowed to access. Many of the operating system modules, are required to execute instructions that application programs cannot execute, and some modules must reference memory areas forbidden to normal programs (they must operate in "kernel space" rather than "user space".)

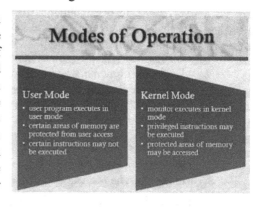

2.1.2 Some OS Programs must Relinquish and Regain Control very Frequently

Most modern computing systems are multiprocessing systems. When an application program begins executing, it is the operating system that transfers control to it, and, in doing so, the operating system must relinquish its control. At some point, the application program must stop. A program might stop because it is done, it might stop to pause, waiting for an I/O operation to finish, or it might stop because it finished its allotted time slice. For whatever reason, when the application program stops, control must return to the operating system. An OS program called the *monitor* will begin to execute. The

---

from other operating system architectures (such as the microkernel architecture) in that it alone defines a high-level virtual interface over computer hardware. A set of primitives or system calls implement all operating system services such as process management, concurrency, and memory management. Device drivers can be added to the kernel as modules (see chapter 3.)

monitor will then identify a process that would be appropriate to execute and pass control to that process.

Application programs can (and often do) relinquish control, only to resume execution later. Few application programs, however, will ever do so as frequently as does *any* operating system monitor.

2.1.3 OS Programs Must Be Efficient

Very few programs execute as frequently as do many of the operating system programs, and, hence, any inefficiencies in the execution of these programs will tend to slow the system much more than would inefficiencies in a program of another type. In particular, it is essential that the transfer of control be done efficiently, since this activity occurs with great frequency (see 2.1.2 above) and any inefficiencies in the process would result in significant slowdowns of system operation.

2.1.4 OS Programs Must Be Reliable

As noted above, operating system programs execute very frequently. Since they execute frequently, any programming errors in them will occur more frequently than will errors in other types of programs. In addition, other programs depend on OS programs to function, and so errors will affect the execution of the other programs too, and not just the individual OS program containing the error. Finally, OS programs are permitted wider range of memory access than are common programs and they can use commands not allowed in common application programs. An error in an OS program would have much greater potential for doing serious damage than would a similar error in a normal application program.

2.1.5 Some OS Programs cannot be Swapped Out to Virtual Memory

The monitor/kernel handles all interrupts. An interrupt can occur at any time, and so the monitor must be resident in RAM at all times.

The monitor is not the only OS program that must remain resident at all times (but it is probably the most obvious example of a program that must remain resident.)

2.2 An OS Must Function as a Resource Manager

Application programs are (generally) resource *users*. The operating system, on the other hand, functions as the resource *manager*[vii].

A computing system will typically have a limited number of resources[10], and quite often there will be several processes running concurrently.

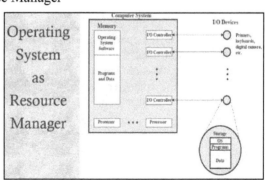

---

[10] Some examples of resources are processors, primary storage, peripherals, secondary storage, and data

When several processes are executing simultaneously, it is pretty much inevitable that two of them will attempt to access some system resource at the same time. Many of these system resources, however, can only be used by one process at a time, and so some control must be exercised over which process gets to use the resource. This is another of the responsibilities of the operating system There must be some system/policy established to govern how the system resources are to be allocated, and the OS must implement/enforce the policy.

2.2.1   Factors in Resource Allocation Policy

Among the factors that must be considered in the design of resource allocation policies are fairness, differential responsiveness and efficiency. Resources should also be allocated in a manner that will avoid "deadlock" and "starvation". These factors/objectives are not necessarily mutually consistent. Different operating systems will give some of the objectives different priorities, depending on what kind of computing systems they are designed for.

2.2.1.1   Fairness

In this context, "fairness" would mean that resources should be allocated in such a way that all processes would have a reasonable expectation of obtaining the resources they need in a reasonable time.

Of course *all* operating systems *should* be "fair" in the above sense. An operating system should never permit "starvation" (see below) but the term "reasonable time" is subject to interpretation and will vary from one situation to another. What one user would consider "fair" is not necessarily what another user would consider "fair". What would be considered a "reasonable" waiting time on a batch system is probably not what an interactive user would consider a "reasonable" waiting time.

2.2.1.2   Responsiveness

In a time sharing system with online users, resources should be allocated in such a way that the *online* users should have a reasonable expectation of system interaction in what they might consider a "reasonable"[11] time.

Again, "reasonable time" is subject to interpretation. In many batch processing systems, for many kinds of processes, a few hours might well be considered "reasonable", whereas on a personal computer or on a system whose users do most of their work online, the Kemeny Kurtz standard of 10 seconds would probably be considered very much too long today.

---

[11]   When designing DTSS (the first successful large-scale time-sharing system) Kemeny and Kurtz were on record as identifying 10 seconds as the maximum response time

2.2.1.3 Efficiency

In this context, the term "efficiency" would mean that resources should be allocated in a way that they are utilized to their greatest degree possible.

This factor tends to be inconsistent with both fairness and responsiveness, and, if given too high a priority, could lead to "starvation". It does, however, have its place in system allocation policies, especially in design of OS's for systems with resources that are extremely expensive (supercomputers for example.)

2.2.1.4 Avoidance of Deadlock and Starvation

In resource allocation, the OS must deal with the most problematic kinds of conflicts. With concurrent processes competing for the same resources, it is quite possible that after a process has been allocated one resource, it might attempt to access a second resource. If that second resource has already been allocated to a second process, the first process must wait until the second process releases it. Then, however the second process might request access to the first resource and the second process will have to wait for the first process to release that resource. At this point, neither process can proceed. If neither process will release its resource until it has finished its task, then neither will ever be able to finish because each requires a resource that the other will not release. Such a situation is called a *deadlock*[viii].

Deadlock condition or situation

Requested   Allocated   Deadlocked

In the above diagram there are two process **P1** and **p2** and there are two resources **R1** and **R2**.

Resource **R1** is allocated to process **P1** and resource **R2** is allocated to process **p2**. To complete execution of process **P1** needs resource **R2**, so **P1** request for **R2**, but **R2** is already allocated to **P2**.

In the same way Process **P2** to complete its execution needs **R1**, but **R1** is already allocated to **P1**

Another, more subtle kind of problem can occur in a busy system when a process needs a commonly used resource, but cannot access it because other, higher priority processes are continually using it. This kind of situation is called *starvation*.

Operating systems must be designed to identify potential deadlock and starvation situations and prevent them from occurring. If one of these situations does occur, the system must recognize the fact and deal with it (and quickly, if that is at all possible.)

2.3 Chapter 2 Exercises

2.3.1 How important would support for portability be in the design of an operating system for personal computers? Why do you think it would be important or unimportant? How do your arguments apply to smartphones?

2.3.2 Does the existence of a large number of drivers for a wide range of devices result in making popular operating systems complex or does it result in permitting the underlying OS to remain relatively simple?

2.3.3 Today the monolithic kernel is the most popular form of kernel design. Can you suggest why it might be more popular than other forms? Can you suggest what kinds of systems the microkernel form might be more appropriate?

2.3.4 The monitor must remain resident in RAM at all times while the system is running. Can you suggest any other types of OS software that must always be resident in memory and should never be swapped out?

2.3.5 Operating systems are generally resource managers while application programs tend to be resource users. Can you suggest any type of application programs that function as resource managers? How does this function affect the interaction between the application and the OS?

2.4 Chapter 2 Questions

2.4.1 True-False

2.4.1.1 Because of the limited memory available, operating systems used on small devices are necessarily quite complex.

2.4.1.2 A kernel connects the application software to the hardware of a computer.

2.4.1.3 The critical code of the kernel is usually loaded into a separate area of memory, which is protected from access by application programs or other, less critical parts of the operating system.

2.4.1.4 Kernel designs differ in how they manage these system calls and resources. A monolithic kernel runs all the operating system instructions in the same address space for speed. A microkernel runs most processes in user space, for modularity. Today, microkernels are the most popular.

2.4.1.5 The monolithic model differs from other operating system architectures in that it alone defines a high-level virtual interface over computer hardware.

2.4.1.6 Because OS programs have more restrictions on the memory they can access than do application programs, an error in an OS program would have less potential for doing serious damage than would a similar error in a normal application program.

2.4.1.7 Among the factors that must be considered in the design of resource allocation policies are: fairness, differential responsiveness and efficiency. Resources should also be allocated in a manner that avoids "deadlocks" and "starvation". These objectives are not necessarily mutually consistent.

2.4.1.8 Efficiency: Resources should be allocated in a way that resources are utilized to their greatest degree possible.
This factor tends to be inconsistent with both fairness and responsiveness.

2.4.2   Multiple Choice

2.4.2.1 A computing system requires a set of resources for the _____ of data
   a.   processing
   b.   moving
   c.   storing
   d   all of the above
   e.   none of the above

2.4.2.2 When a process makes requests of the kernel, it is called a _____
   a.   service request
   b.   system call
   c.   kernel call
   d.   core request
   e.   none of the above

2.4.2.3 Most modern computing systems are _____ systems
   a.   batch
   b.   application
   c.   multiprocessing
   d.   multiuser
   e.   none of the above

2.4.2.4 Resources should be allocated in a way that all processes should have a reasonable expectation of obtaining the resources they need in a reasonable time. This factor that must be considered in the design of resource allocation policies is the factor of
   _____
   a.   fairness
   b.   differential responsiveness
   c.   efficiency
   d.   all of the above
   e.   none of the above

2.4.3   Completion

2.4.3.1 A computing system requires a set of _____ for the processing, moving and storing of data.

2.4.3.2 A(n) _____ is a shared boundary across which two or more separate components of a computer system exchange information.

2.4.3.3 The _____ is a computer program that is the core of a computer's operating system, with complete control over everything in the system.

2.4.3.4 Kernel designs differ in how they manage these system calls and resources. A(n) _____ kernel runs all the operating system instructions in the same address space for speed.

2.4.3.5 A(n) _____ **kernel** is an operating system architecture in which the entire operating system is working in "kernel space" and is alone in supervisor mode.

2.4.3.6 When an application program relinquishes control, the OS program called the _____ begins to execute.

2.4.3.7 Application programs are (generally) resource *users*. The operating system, on the other hand, functions as the resource _____ .

2.4.3.8 When a process needs a commonly used resource, but cannot access it because other, higher priority processes are continually using it, this kind of situation is called _____.

3. Relationships of the Operating System Modules

Although some parts of the operating system must remain resident at all times (the monitor, for example) there are other parts/programs that are can remain in secondary memory until needed and be loaded into RAM when necessary.

Practically speaking the division of the operating system into separate modules that can be loaded dynamically provides a very flexible way of handling an operating system image at runtime. Operating systems are so complex that it is not practical to load the entire system into RAM, with all possible options. The only other alternative, then, would be to reboot the system with a different image whenever additional functionality is required. In addition, the separation of the OS into distinct modules with specific responsibilities makes it relatively easy to extend/upgrade the capabilities of an OS as needed. Dynamically loadable modules incur a small overhead when compared to building all conceivable functionality into the operating system image.

Loading modules dynamically (as needed) helps to keep the amount of code running in kernel space to a minimum. It will reduce operating system footprint to optimum size (especially important for embedded devices or those with limited hardware resources.) Unneeded modules need not be stored in (possibly scarce and/or expensive) random access memory.

An operating system has a number of responsibilities and must perform many varied functions. It is only reasonable that these different activities be executed by separate programs/modules, some of which may be permanently resident (part of the kernel) and some of which may be dynamically loadable (reducing the kernel footprint, as mentioned earlier.) This type of organization simplifies (somewhat) the design of what is (as mentioned earlier) one of the most complex types of programs in the history of the computing industry. It also simplifies updating the OS, since with this configuration an update might only require that a portion of the code (one or two modules) be modified.

Among the types of modules involved in an operating system would be:

Process management modules.

Memory management modules:

I/O modules:

3.1 Process Management Modules:

The *process management modules* control which processes are to be allocated for a processor to execute. The process management module includes small processes/programs for switching the processor from one process to another (i.e. for transferring "*control*" from one process to another.)

3.1.1 What is a Process

Recall from 1.2.4.1, a process can be defined as an entity that can be assigned to, and be executed by, a processor. It is a unit of activity characterized by having a single sequential thread of execution, a current state, and an associated set of system resources.

A process contains three components: *executable code*, *associated data* (the data needed by the process variables, work space, buffers, etc.) and the *execution context* (or "process state") of the program.

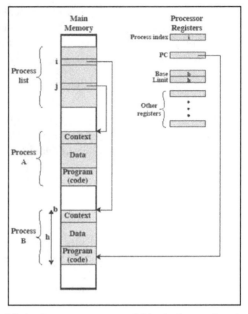

When the processor begins to execute program code, that code must be associated with some entity characterized as a *process*[ix].

While the program/process is executing, the process can be uniquely characterized by a number of elements, including: *identifier, state, priority, program counter, memory pointers, context data, I/O status information* and *accounting by the processor.* There will be a *Process Control Block (PCB)*[x] which contains these process elements and it is the process control block that makes it possible to interrupt a running process and later resume execution as if the interruption had not occurred.

A *PCB* is created and managed by the operating system and is a key tool that allows support for both interrupt processing and multiple concurrent processes.

One of the activities of the process manager is that of handling the removal of a running process from a CPU and the selection of another process for the CPU to begin executing. It is best that this selection process (*process scheduling*) be made on the basis of some strategy. Process scheduling is an essential part of any multiprogramming operating system.

The OS maintains all PCBs in Process Scheduling *Queues*. The system will maintain a separate queue for each of the process states and PCBs of all processes in the same execution state are placed in the same queue. When the state of a process is changed, its PCB is unlinked from its current queue and linked into its new state queue.

The behavior of an individual process can be traced by listing the sequence of instructions that the process executes. The behavior of the processor can be characterized by showing how the traces of the various processes are interleaved.

Process Control Block

There are several different state models. Among them are:
the 2 State Model,
the 5 state Model,
and the 7 State Model.

3.1.1.1 Process States: 2 State Model[xi]

The simplest of the models involves only two states. "Running" and "Not-Running".

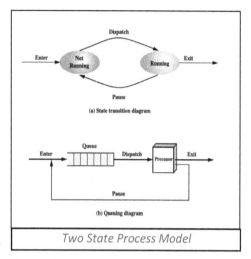

In a system using this model, no process is created unless it can begin executing immediately. Processes are only entered into the system when they can be entered in the "Running" state.

In this system, when a running process is interrupted, it is transferred to the "Not-Running" queue, unless it finished running or aborted. In either of these two cases, the execution of the process would be stopped and a process would be selected from the "Not-Running" queue to start executing.

3.1.1.2 Process States: 5 State Model[xii]

The 5 state model is probably the most commonly used state model:

Five-State Process Model: A process may be in one of five distinct states:
1. *Created/New*: The process has been loaded in memory but has not yet been entered into either the "waiting" queue of processes ready to be executed or the list of "Blocked" processes waiting for some event to free them for execution.

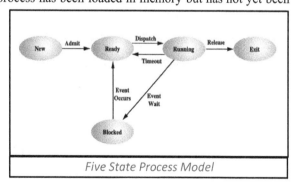

Five State Process Model

2. *Ready:* The process is in memory and is in the "waiting" queue, waiting to be assigned to a processor to be executed
3. *Running:* The process is being executed by a processor.
4. *Blocked:* The process is waiting for some event (such as: I/O completion, allocation of a resource, etc.)
5. *Exit:* The process has already finished its task.

31

3.1.1.3 Process States: 7 State Model[xiii]

In systems that have virtual memory, two additional states are available:

swapped out and waiting

swapped out and blocked

In both of these additional states, processes are "stored" on secondary memory (typically a hard disk).

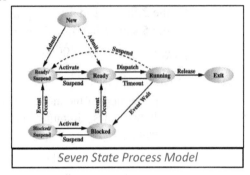

Seven State Process Model

3.1.1.3.1 **Swapped Out and Waiting**

(Also called **suspended and waiting**.) In systems that support virtual memory, a process may be swapped out, that is, removed from main memory and placed on external storage by the scheduler. From here the process may be swapped back into the waiting state.

3.1.1.3.2 **Swapped Out and Blocked**

(Also called **suspended and blocked**.) Processes that are blocked may also be swapped out. In this event the process is both swapped out and blocked, and may be swapped back in again under the same circumstances as a swapped out and waiting process (although in this case, the process will move to the blocked state, and may still be waiting for a resource to become available).

3.1.1.4 Changing Process States

There are a number of reasons that a "Running" process might stop:

its time slice might have finished;

it might have paused to wait for an I/O operation to complete;

it might have stopped to issue a request to spawn a new process;

it might have finished its task;

it might have been preempted by a higher priority process (a notification that an I/O operation has finished would be a common example);

it might have reached a point where it needs some additional system resource;

it might have stopped for some other reason.

3.1.1.4.1 Process States and Interrupts

If the running process stops, for whatever reason, control must be transferred to another process. The CPU cannot just stop operating, it must execute SOME instruction.

When a process stops, an interrupt must be involved. It is possible that it was an externally generated interrupt that stopped the process. It is also possible that the process itself generated the interrupt (possibly signaling an I/O request, a request to spawn a new process, termination of its task, ...) Whatever its the source, the interrupt will include the information the system needs to determine what to do next.

The *system monitor* is the process/program that starts executing whenever an interrupt occurs. The monitor, then, will choose another appropriate process (based on the information provided by the interrupt) and set the processor to start executing that process.

In general, whenever an interrupt occurs, control transfers to the monitor. The monitor determines what kind of interrupt caused it to start running and takes appropriate action to respond to that interrupt.

3.1.1.4.2 Process States: Time Slice Interrupts

If the original process stopped because its time slice expired, the monitor will choose a process that changes the state of the original process from "R*unning*" to "W*aiting*". It will then put that process in the queue of waiting processes, choose a process from the "*waiting*" queue, change the state of that process to "R*unning*" and transfer control to it.

3.1.1.4.3 Process States: I/O Operation Interrupts

If the original process stopped because it was requesting some I/O operation, then the monitor/kernel must change the state of the process to "*Blocked*", put the process in the list of "*Blocked*" *processes,* and start the I/O module process for dealing with this kind of I/O request. The actual I/O operation will normally be done by equipment not under direct control of the CPU (I/O operations tend to be much slower than those controlled by a CPU, and so would slow the computer to an inacceptable degree if handled directly.) The process from the I/O module will start the I/O equipment running and return control to the monitor. The monitor will then select a process from the "*waiting*" queue, set its state to "running" and start it executing.

3.1.1.4.4 Process States: Spawning a New Process

On occasion, a running process will need to create (and execute) another (new) process. The procedure that must be followed, in this case, is rather similar to that of an I/O request, but instead of using a process from the I/O module, the monitor will choose a "*new process creation process*" from the process management module. A new process will be created, the process creation process will deal with the state and queue position of the new process, and control will be returned to the monitor. The monitor will then select and start a process from the waiting queue.

3.1.1.4.5 Process States: Task Termination

If a process finishes its task, it will issue the appropriate interrupt, and, in response, the kernel will initiate the appropriate *"process termination"* process from the process management module. This process will reclaim the process resources and then return control to the monitor so that it can select a process from the waiting queue.

3.1.1.4.6 Process States: Task Preemption

The execution of a process can be stopped by interrupts generated by external equipment (most often the I/O system.)

If the I/O system completes an operation it will issue an interrupt. The monitor will identify the process that requested the original I/O operation, change the state of that process from *blocked* to *waiting*, put it in the waiting queue and return control to the process that had been running when the I/O interrupt occurred.

3.1.2 Process Scheduling

Process schedulers are special system software that handle process scheduling in various ways. Their main tasks are to select the jobs to be submitted into the system , to move processes from one queue to another, and to decide which process to run. There are three types of schedulers:

Short-Term Schedulers; Long-Term Schedulers; Medium-Term Schedulers

3.1.2.1 Short-Term Schedulers

Short-Term Schedulers (*CPU schedulers*) have, as their main objective to increase system performance (in accordance with some chosen set of criteria.) A CPU scheduler selects a process from among the processes in the "waiting" queue and allocates CPU to it.

3.1.2.2 Long Term Schedulers

Long Term Schedulers are also called *job schedulers*. A long term scheduler determines which programs are admitted to the system for processing. It selects processes from the "created" queue, loads them into memory for execution and inserts them into either the "waiting" or "blocked" queue as appropriate.

The primary objective of the job scheduler is to provide a balanced mix of jobs, some I/O bound and some compute bound. It also controls the degree of multiprogramming. For the degree of multiprogramming to be stable, the average rate of process creation must be equal to the average departure rate of processes leaving the system.

Some systems may have no long-term scheduler, or only a very minimal one. Many time-sharing operating systems will have no long term scheduler. On these systems, a process automatically changes state from new to ready.

3.1.2.3 Medium Term Scheduler

Medium-term scheduling is a part of the virtual memory process. It moves the processes from primary to secondary memory, and returns them from secondary to primary memory, as needed.

A running process may become suspended. This will happen most commonly if it makes an I/O request. A suspended process cannot make any progress towards completion. Processes in this condition can be moved from primary memory to secondary storage to make space in RAM for other processes. This process is called swapping, and the process is said to be swapped out or rolled out.

A medium-term scheduler identifies which processes to swap out and swap back in.

3.2 Memory management module:

Memory management is the function responsible for managing the computer's primary memory. The memory management function keeps track of the status of each memory location, whether it is *allocated* or *free*. It also determines how memory is allocated among different processes. It decides which process gets memory, when it gets it, how much it gets, and what memory it gets.

When memory is to be allocated, memory management determines which memory locations will be assigned. It also tracks when memory is freed (*deallocated*) and updates the status of those memory locations.

At its core then, the memory manager has the task of allocating memory to each job/process to be executed and of reclaiming the memory whenever a process completes, or, for some other reason, releases memory.

In any system, an application program must be restricted as to what areas of memory it can access. Even in the simplest single user single process batch systems, the operating system code must be protected from being overwritten by an application process, so the "memory allocation" referred to above, implies some form of system control over the memory allocated to, used by, and accessible from each of the processes.

In multiprogramming systems, decisions must be made concerning where a given program will be loaded into memory and, once loaded, what areas it can access. Then, these limitations must be enforced.

The memory manager will check the validity of each request for memory space, and, if it is a legal request, will allocate a section of unused RAM. The manager will maintain a table keeping track of what sections are allocated to what processes. Note that this is complicated by the fact that, although the memory used by distinct processes will normally be nonoverlapping, there will be situations (buffers used in synchronization of concurrent processes for example) in which two processes might need to reference the same memory. It is the responsibility of the memory management system to keep track of and enforce the process reference rights.

In systems supporting virtual memory and/or cache memory, the memory manager will typically set up tables to keep track of which sections of memory are allocated to which processes, which blocks are associated with which blocks of cache, which process pages have been swapped out to which pages of virtual memory (and will issue commands to the I/O system to retrieve an appropriate virtual page, in the event that a process should reference something swapped out.)

3.3   I/O Module

The I/O Module provides a system for exchanging data between processors and external I/O devices.

3.3.1   Types of I/O modules

There are several types of I/O module. A few of the most common are described below:

3.3.1.1   Programmed I/O

Programmed I/O is the simplest I/O technique for exchanging data between a processor and an external device.

With *Programmed I/O*, the processor executes a program that takes the direct control of I/O operation. The processor issues a command to the I/O device and waits until the operation is complete. The processor must periodically check the status of I/O module until it finds that the operation has completed.

3.3.1.2   Interrupt-driven I/O

Interrupt driven I/O has many features in common with Programmed I/O, but with this technique, the processor does not stop and wait for the I/O operation to complete. Instead, after issuing a command to an I/O device controller, it continues on to process other tasks. When the I/O operation has finished, the I/O device will issue an interrupt and the processor will pause its operations and process the I/O interrupt.

3.3.1.3   DMA I/O

[xiv]DMA is an acronym for *Direct Memory Access*. DMA I/O modules exchange data directly between memory and I/O devices without any involvement of a CPU.

DMA I/O produces fast data transfer rates because there is the transfer is independent of any other process that the CPU might be executing.

With DMA, the CPU first initiates the transfer, issuing commands to the DMA controller the commands will identify devices, and memory buffer in RAM to be used. Then it goes on with other operations while the data transfer is in progress. Finally, when the data transfer operation is done, the DMA controller emits an interrupt. This feature is especially useful in situations where the CPU cannot keep up with the rate of data transfer, or when the CPU needs to perform work while waiting for a relatively slow I/O data transfer. Many hardware systems use DMA, including disk drive controllers, graphics cards, network cards and sound cards. The DMA controller uses the data bus to make its transfers to and from main memory. Since its activities are independent of those of the CPU, the times it can use this bus must be coordinated with data transfers by the CPU.

DMA I/O differs from the above described interrupt driven I/O in that with interrupt driven I/O, the CPU must deal with the device controller directly, copying data into or out of the controller, whereas with DMA I/O, the DMA controller does all the data transfer into or out of RAM.

3.3.2 I/O Module Functions: [12]

The I/O module is responsible for moving data between the computer and external environments, (external peripheral devices.)

External devices generally have characteristics very different from those of internal memory (different response rates, different word sizes, ...) so some form of interface is required between these devices and computer memory (so that the programs executing on a CPU can have some way to interact with the external devices.)

An I/O module (a device manager) manages communication with peripheral devices. It must balance supply and demand, and enforce policies dictated by device characteristics, as well as system load situations and local system priorities.

The primary functions and responsibilities of an I/O module would be:

Control and timing

Processor communication

Device communication

Data buffering

Error detection

3.3.2.1 Control and Timing:

When transferring data to or from RAM, communication with the external environment will generally use the same data buses that are used in the execution of normal programs. Of course, I/O transfer cannot take place at the same time that the CPU is moving data to or from RAM as part of its execution of a program. An I/O control unit must transfer data from a buffer to a device or from a device to a buffer only at a time when the processor(s) will not be moving data to or from locations in RAM.

---

[12]   This section is taken largely from "Computer Organization and Architecture Designing for Performance" by William Stallings

3.3.2.2 Processor Communication

Processor communication involves:

Command Decoding: The I/O module receives commands from the processor (these commands will be transmitted on the control bus.) It identifies the commands and any parameters.

Data: Data to be stored on external device, or data retrieved from external device. The data is exchanged between I/O module and processor. This exchange is done using the data bus.

Status reporting: The I/O module reports on the module state. (Possible states are READY, BUSY, ERROR) The processor executing the process doing I/O must be able to determine whether/when to send/receive another unit of data.

Address recognition: The I/O module will often control more than one external device and so the module must recognize a unique address for each of the devices with which it interfaces.

3.3.2.3 Device Communication

The I/O module interfaces with and controls external data storage devices, and so it must, then be able to:

send commands to each device

determine the status of any device

send or receive data to/from each device

3.3.2.4 Data Buffering

The data transfer rate in and out of main memory will in general be very different from that of an external device. (Most of these devices are much slower, but a few are much faster.) External devices also tend to send and receive data in standardized amounts (one byte at a time, one word at a time, one page at a time, etc.) and the input sizes do not necessarily match the output sizes (the processor might be sending data one byte at a time, but the hard disk uses data a sector of 512 bytes at a time.)

The I/O module must receive input data and store it until there is a sufficient amount and the receiving unit is ready to receive it.

3.3.2.5 Error Detection

I/O Modules are often responsible for error detection and, subsequently, reporting these errors so that the system might deal with them. Data transmission and storage usually incorporate some kind of error detection strategies to identify when (and if possible what kinds of) errors have occurred, either in storage or transmission. These detection strategies often involve parity bits. For more information on error detection, see chapter 8.

3.4 Exercises

3.4.1 Explain how a process is different from a program.

3.4.2 In what kind of computing system would you be more likely to find an operating system using the two state model process of allocation?

3.5 Chapter 3 Questions

3.5.1 True-False

3.5.1.1 One of the disadvantages of dynamically loadable modules is their relatively large I/O overhead when compared to building all conceivable functionality into the operating system image.

3.5.1.2 Different activities can be executed by separate programs/modules. Some of the modules may be permanently resident (part of the kernel) and some may be dynamically loadable.

3.5.1.3 The OS maintains all PCBs in the **Process Scheduling Queue (PSQ).**

3.5.1.4 If a running process stops, the CPU will pause until another process can be selected to receive control.

3.5.1.5 There are several types of I/O module.

3.5.1.6 Most external devices generally have characteristics very similar to those of internal memory.

3.5.1.7 Communication with the external environment will generally use the same data buses that are used in the execution of normal programs.

3.5.1.8 An I/O module will often control more than one external device and so the module must recognize a unique address for each of the devices with which it interfaces.

3.5.1.9 Data transmission and storage usually incorporate some kind of error detection strategies to identify when and (if possible) what kinds errors have occurred, either in storage or transmission. These detection strategies often involve parity bits.

3.5.2 Multiple Choice

3.5.2.1 Using dynamically loadable modules _____
    a.   helps to keep the amount of code running in kernel space to a minimum.
    b.   will reduce operating system footprint to optimum size
    c.   allows for easy extension/upgrading of the operating system
    d.   all of the above
    e.   none of the above

3.5.2.2　While the program/process is executing, the process can be uniquely characterized by a number of elements, including: *identifier, state, priority, program counter, memory pointers, context data, I/O status information* and *accounting by the processor.* There will be a _____ which contains these process elements

   a.　　*Process Assignment Block (PAB)*
   b.　　*Process Assignment Table (PAT)*
   c.　　*Process Control Block (PCB)*
   d.　　*Process Control Table (PCT)*
   e.　　none of the above

3.5.2.3　Possibly the most commonly used state model is the _____ model

   a.　　one state
   b.　　two state
   c.　　five state
   d.　　seven state
   e.　　none of the above

3.5.2.4　A(n) _____ scheduler has, as its main objective to increase system performance (in accordance with some chosen set of criteria.) It selects a process from among the processes in the "waiting" queue to be allocated a CPU

   a.　　short term
   b.　　long term
   c.　　medium term
   d.　　interrupt processing
   e.　　none of the above

3.5.2.5　In systems with cache memory and/or virtual memory, the memory manager will typically set up _____ to keep track of which sections of memory are allocated to which processes, which are associated with sections of cache and which processes involve what kind of sections of virtual memory.

   a.　　lists
   b.　　queues
   c.　　tables
   d.　　stacks
   e.　　none of the above

3.5.2.6　With _____ I/O the processor will periodically check the status of I/O module until it finds that the operation has completed.

   a.　　Programmed
   b.　　Interrupt Driven
   c.　　DMA
   d.　　Modular
   e.　　none of the above

3.5.2.7　A hardware system that might use DMA would be a _____

   a.　　disk drive controller
   b.　　sound card
   c.　　network card
   d.　　all of the above
   e.　　none of the above

3.5.3 Completion

3.5.3.1 Division of the system into dynamically loadable _____ is a very flexible way of handling an operating system image at runtime (as opposed to rebooting with a different operating system image whenever additional functionality might be required.)

3.5.3.2 A process is a unit of activity characterized by having a single sequential _____ of execution, a current state, and an associated set of system resources.

3.5.3.3 A process is a unit of activity characterized by having a single sequential thread of execution, a current state, and an associated set of system _____.

3.5.3.4 In a two state model system, processes are only entered into the system when they can be entered in the "_____" state.

3.5.3.5 In a five (or seven) state model system, a process is said to be in the _____ state if it is in memory and is in the "waiting" queue, waiting to be assigned to a processor to be executed.

3.5.3.6 When a process stops, a(n) _____ will be generated.

3.5.3.7 For the degree of _____ to be stable, the average rate of process creation must be equal to the average departure rate of processes leaving the system.

3.5.3.8 The I/O Module is a system for exchanging data between processors and _____ I/O devices.

3.5.3.9 DMA is an acronym for _____ _Memory Access._

3.5.3.10 External devices generally have characteristics very different from those of internal memory (different response rates, different word sizes, ...) so some form of _____ is required between these devices and computer memory.

4. Concurrent Processes and Synchronization, Deadlocks and Starvation

All modern operating systems have to deal with the problems of concurrent processes (processes dealing with things that are going on simultaneously.) Even the systems on the simplest single user personal computers must control the display on the monitor and deal with user input from keyboard and/or mouse concurrently with the execution of any of the user's application programs.

In fact, computing systems have evolved to where most modern systems involve more than one processor (are *multiprocessor* systems), and so, while older single processor systems can give the *impression* of concurrent processing (using time slicing to permit several processes to share access to the processor) multiprocessor systems really do involve genuinely concurrent processing, i.e. multiple processes are executing at exactly the same time (on different processors.)

When multiple processes are active at the same time, it is common that some of them will need to interact (one process providing information needed by another, one process determining the state of another, …). The interaction and synchronization of concurrent processes can become extremely subtle and complex Concurrency also creates the possibility of deadlock and/or starvation (as mentioned earlier, in section 2.2.1.4.)

4.1 Process Interaction/Synchronization

The way that concurrent processes communicate with each other is typically by leaving data/messages in commonly accessible memory locations (buffers.)

When concurrent processes can access common memory, however, many things can go wrong. "Synchronization" is a very complex issue and is subject to very subtle errors that can be extremely difficult to debug.

Nevertheless, synchronization is essential for concurrency to work.

4.1.1 Simple Producer-Consumer (Reader-Writer)

Consider a situation in which there are two processes, Prd and Cns, and each can access the same buffer Buf. Process Prd produces values and stores them in Buf to be used by Cns. Process Cns reads values from Buf and uses them for something (think of Cns as a printer driver and Prd as a process in a word processing program which stores text characters in Buf, and Cns a process to send text to a printer.)

Cns should not try to read a value from Buf until after Prd has placed a value there, and Prd should never try to store a new value in Buf until after Cns has removed any previous values. (We assume there can be only one instance of each procedure.)

One might be tempted to deal with this situation using the following combination of procedures:

```
procedure Prd(parVal)
    if ( Buf<>null ) pauseProcedure(Prd)
    Buf = parVal
    startProcedure( Cns )
    endProcedure(Prd)
```

```
procedure Cns()
    useValue(Buf)
    Buf=null
    if pausedProcedure ( Prd ) resumeProcedure( Prd )
    endProcedure(Cns)
```

The above pair of procedures DOES look like it should work.

When the main program starts, buffer Buf would initially contain null.
Some external process would provide a value for the parameter *parVal* and initiates execution of procedure Prd(*parVal*).
Since Buf contains null, Prd does not pause, and *parVal* is stored in Buf. Procedure Cns begins to execute and procedure Prd terminates.
Procedure Cns might complete (process the value in Buf, set Buf to null and, if procedure Prd is not in a paused state, Cns terminates) and nothing more happens until Prd is executed again.

It *might*, however, be the case that Prd would be reinitiated before Cns completes its action.

a) Possibly procedure Cns has not yet set Buf to null at the time that procedure Prd evaluates the expression (Buf<>null). In this case, procedure Prd will pause, procedure Cns will continue. It will set Buf to null, and, since Prd is paused, Cns will resume Prd. and terminate. (Note that, since only one instance of Cns is allowed, Prd cannot execute startProcedure(Cns) until Cns has terminated.)

b) If procedure Cns were to have executed (Buf=null) when Prd comes to have evaluated (Buf<>null) then Prd would not pause. It will store its new parameter value in Buf and attempt to execute startProcedure(Cns) Meanwhile Cns will not execute resumeProcedure(Prd). but instead simply terminate and at this point, Prd will be able to execute startProcedure(Cns) and will, terminate, and do nothing more until such time as the external process provides a new parVal and restarts procedure Prd.

c) The PROBLEM with the above construct is that (assuming, of course, that Prd and Cns are concurrent) the following scenario might conceivably occur:

    1. Prd evaluates (Buf<>null) before Cns sets Buf to null
    2. Before Prd can execute pauseProcedure(Prd), Cns continues, sets Buf to null, and then
    3. Since pausedProcedure(Prd) is not true, Cns does not execute resumeProcedure(Prd) but simply continues on to its termination, endProcedure(Cns)
    4. At this point Prd executes pauseProcedure(Prd)
    5. This leaves the system deadlocked, with a paused Prd and a nonexecuting Cns. Cns can only be restarted by Prd, but the paused Prd can only be resumed by Cns.

44

External process		Prd	Cns	Buf
		inactive	inactive	null
Prd(v1)		active	inactive	null
	Prd:(Buf<>null) is false	active	inactive	null
	Prd:(Buf=v1)	active	inactive	v1
	Prd:(startProcedure(Cns))	active	active	v1
	Prd:(endProcedure(Prd))	inactive	active	v1
Prd(v2)		active	active	v1
	Prd:(Buf<>null) is true	active	active	v1
	Cns:(useValue(Buf))	active	active	v1
	Cns:(Buf=null)	active	active	null
	Cns:(Prd not paused)	active	active	null
	Cns:(endProcedure(Cns))	active	inactive	null
	Prd:(pauseProcedure(Prd))	paused	inactive	null
Sequence leading to deadlocked Producer-Consumer 4.1.1				

4.1.2 Critical Regions

The example in 4.1.1 is typical of many synchronization situations. One way to avoid this kind of problem, is to ensure that any nontrivial process, once initiated, must be allowed to complete, before others can be allowed to continue.

In the case of 4.1.1 the process that must complete is
  if (B<>null) pauseProcedure(P)

The common element of all (successful) synchronization schemes is a ***critical region*** whose execution must be handled as a unit without being interleaved with the execution of others.

Several mechanisms have been developed to implement critical regions. Among the most common are "*test-and-set*" and "*semaphores*":

> *test-and-set*: Test-and-set was first introduced by IBM for its 360/370 computers. The **test-and-set** instruction is a hardware instruction used to write the value 1 to a memory location ("set" the memory location) and return the value originally in the memory location, both actions executed as a single atomic (i.e., non-interruptible) operation. If multiple processes may access the same memory location, and if a process is currently performing a test-and-set, no other process may begin another test-and-set (or in any other way access the memory location being "tested") until the first process's test-and-set is finished. (Note that implementation can be problematic on shared memory multiprocessor systems.)

semaphores: A semaphore is a nonnegative integer variable used as a flag. The variable, together with two uninterruptible unary operators, (traditionally identified as **P**, to test and decrement the value in the variable, and **V**, to increment the value in the variable[13]) form an abstract data type that is often used for access control to common resources used by multiple processes in concurrent systems.

The semaphore concept was invented by Dutch computer scientist Edsger Dijkstra in 1962 or 1963.

There are two types of semaphores, counting semaphores and binary semaphores.

4.1.2.1 Binary Semaphores

For a binary semaphore, the variable is restricted to the values 0 and 1. Binary semaphores are typically used to create/implement mutually exclusive critical regions (mutexes)

If S is a binary semaphore and a process attempts to execute P(S)

If the value of S is 1, then S is set to 0 and the process is allowed to continue (note that the operation P is atomic/uninterruptible, so no process can intervene between the testing of S being 1 or 0 and the modification of its value.)

If the value of S is 0, then the process is not allowed to proceed, but will be required to try executing P(S) again. The process might just be returned to the ready queue to wait for another turn, but more often it will be placed in the blocked queue, to be returned to the ready queue when the value of S changes to 1)

If S is a binary semaphore and a process executes V(S)

The value of S will be set to 1.

If S has an associated queue of blocked processes and this queue is not empty, one of the processes will be removed and returned to the ready queue, so that it can once again attempt to execute P(S)

4.1.2.2 Counting Semaphores

For a counting semaphore, the variable can take any nonnegative integer value. Counting semaphores are often used to keep track of the number of units of some type of resource in a system available for allocation.

If S is a counting semaphore and a process attempts to execute P(S)

If the value of S is 0, then, just as with binary semaphores, the process is not allowed to proceed, but will be required to try executing P(S) again. The process might just be returned to the ready queue to wait for another turn, but more often it will be placed

---

[13] The letters P and V are from the Dutch *proberen* (to test) and *verhogen* (to increment. The original designer of semaphores was Dutch, after all.

in the blocked queue, to be returned to the ready queue when the value of S becomes nonnegative)

If the value of S is greater than 0, then the value of S will be decremented, and the process will be allowed to continue (note that the operation P is atomic/uninterruptible, so no process can intervene between the testing of S being 0 and the modification of its value.)

If S is a counting semaphore and a process executes V(S), the value in S will be incremented, and, if S has a nonempty queue of blocked processes they will be removed and reassigned to the ready queue so they can attempt to execute P(S) again.

4.1.2.3 Wait and Signal

The P and V operators are often described in terms of *wait* and *signal* actions

- **wait**:
  If the value in the semaphore variable is positive, decrement it by 1 and allow the process to continue.
  If the value in the semaphore variable is 0, the process executing the wait operator is blocked, not allowed to proceed (required to *wait*) until the semaphore's value has become positive.

- **signal**:
  Increments the value of semaphore variable by 1 (or just sets it to 1 in case of a binary semaphore) then, if the semaphore has any blocked processes, allow one of them to attempt to execute the wait operation again (*signal* the system that another resource has become available.)

4.1.3 Producer-Consumer (Reader-Writer) using Semaphores

Consider, again, the situation with two processes, Prd and Cns, each of which can access the same buffer Buf. Process Prd produces values and stores them in Buf to be used by Cns. Process Cns reads values from Buf and *uses/consumes* them (in some way that we don't have to be really specific about.).

Cns should not try to read a value from Buf until after Prd has placed a value there, and Prd should not try to store a new value in Buf until after Cns has removed any previous values. In this example, we will use two semaphores (*writer*, initialized to 1, and *reader*, initialized to 0.)

We can deal with the producer-consumer situation (described above) using the following combination of procedures:

```
procedure Prd(parVal)
    P(writer)
    Buf = parVal
    startProcedure(Cns)
    V(reader)
    endProcedure(Prd)
```

```
procedure Cns()
    P(reader)
    useValue(Buf)
    V(writer)
endProcedure(Cns).
```

With this pair, when the external process provides a value *Parval* and executes
Prd(*Parval*). The semaphore procedure P(writer) sets writer to 0, so any further attempts to
execute W will be blocked until V(writer) is executed.

Next, Prd executes Buf=*Parval*, and then startProcedure(Cns). The first command in Cns is
P(reader), but reader was initialized to 0, so Cns can proceed no further until V(reader) has
been executed.

We don't want Cns to procced until procedure Prd has stored a value in Buf. Only after it
does so, will Prd execute V(*reader*). At this point, further attempts by processes to execute
Prd will be blocked by semaphore *writer* and will remain blocked until after Cns has
processed the value in B and executed V(writer)

The sequence Prd:P(writer) ... Prd: startProcedure(Cns) ... Cns:V(writer) establishes a
critical region in which no new instance of procedure Prd can begin executing

Similarly, (although probably of less importance for this situation) the sequence
Cns:P(reader) ... Prd:V(reader) establishes another critical region, this one making sure that
only one instance of Cns can be accessing Buf at any one time.

4.1.4 More Complex Producer-Consumer

Consider, now a more complex system, a system having more than one buffer in order to
store multiple values. A system might have a number of resources, each of which can be
assigned/allocated to only one process at a time (and, of course deallocated as the process
finishes with it. As an example, consider the various memory pages of RAM in a paging
memory system.) A multiprogramming system would be expected to involve multiple
processes and each process might well be allocated multiple resources.

For this kind of situation, we could begin by representing the resources by entries in an array
resourceArray[ ]. Each entry in the array is associated with a specific resource. The values
of the entries in *resourceArray* will identify which processes, if any, the resources are
allocated to, and so would include a field of type we will designate as *"processID"*. The
values of these fields will all be initially be set to *null* (to indicate that the resource is not
assigned to any process.)

We will use three semaphores, two counting semaphores *Allocated* (initialized to 0) and
Available (initialized to *Max*, the number of entries in the array, and the number of resources
the system has) and one binary semaphore *Mutex*[14] (initialized to 1).

---

[14] Mutex is a name traditionally assigned to a semaphore used for mutual exclusion. MUtual
EXclusion

In our system, we will make use of two functions, *assign()* and *release()*

```
function assign(processID)
    P(Available)
    P(Mutex)
    i=0
    while (resourceArray[i].process<>null)
        i++
    resourceArray[i].process = processID
    V(Mutex)
    return(resourceArray[i].resource)

procedure release(resourceID)
    P(Mutex)
    i=0
    while (resourceArray[i].resource<>resourceID)
        i++
    resourceArray[i].process = null
    V(Mutex)
    V(Available)
```

With this construct, any number of simultaneous processes can attempt to execute function *assign()*. Each attempt will come to P(*Available*) and, if semaphore *Available* is 0, will be blocked and placed in the semaphore's blocked process queue. Because of the initial settings, as many as *Max* processes might successfully execute P(*Available*) and attempt the next command P(*Mutex*). Mutex was initialized at 1, so when the first of the processes executes P(*Mutex*) the semaphore value becomes 0 and all subsequent attempts will be placed in the *Mutex* waiting list. No further instance of *assign()* can execute P(*Mutex*) (nor can nor any instance of *release()* either for that matter) until that first instance of *assign()* has found an unassigned resource and assigned it to its process. Next, *assign* executes V(*Mutex*) which will return the value of the semaphore to 1 and release any processes from its waiting list, so that one of them might succeed in executing P(*Mutex*) and proceed in its path of execution.

Any process, after having been assigned a resource, can later release it, executing the procedure *release*(resourceID), which will make that resource available for reassignment (setting the process field of its *resourceArray[ ]* entry to null) and increasing the count of available resources by executing V(*Available*)

4.2 Deadlock Prevention and Recovery

A deadlock occurs when there are several processes, each of which has some resources assigned, but cannot proceed because they need other resources that cannot be assigned them because they have been assigned to other processes which cannot proceed because they also need other resources which ... and so on.

Preventing/avoiding deadlocks requires that all processes identify all resources they will need before they are allowed to begin running. Any process which requires a resource already committed to an active process would have to wait (with no resources allocated) until all necessary resources have been released by the processes using them. A process would only be released for execution when all necessary resources are available. In early days of computing, when operating systems were batch systems, it was generally possible for programmers to identify all resources that would be needed by a program. With the advent of interactive systems, however, it has become infeasible to require users to identify in advance the resources that they will be using. For one thing, many interactive users are relatively unsophisticated and not really aware of exactly what resources their programs are using.

Even if it were feasible to require all processes to identify all necessary resources, the requirement that all necessary resources be available would often result in unnecessarily slow execution. Most systems, and especially interactive systems, usually make more efficient use of resources through *dynamic* resource sharing. Dynamic resource sharing, however, creates the possibility of a deadlock.

When a deadlock occurs, the only way to recover, is to require a process to release one of the resources involved and allow another process to proceed. Releasing the resource, of course, might result in loss of information on the part of the process releasing that resource. In many systems such data loss can be tolerated, but in many others (especially many real time systems) such data loss could prove disastrous (systems such as hospital life support systems, aircraft guidance systems, …)

4.2.1 Coffman Conditions

A deadlock situation can arise in a system if and only if all of the following conditions hold simultaneously in the system[15]:

1. *Mutual exclusion:* At least one resource must be held in a non-shareable mode. Otherwise, the processes would not be prevented from using the resource when necessary.

2. *Hold and wait* or *resource holding:* a process is currently holding at least one resource and requesting additional resources which are being held by other processes.

3. *No preemption:* a resource can be released only voluntarily by the process holding it.

4. *Circular wait:* each process must be waiting for a resource which is being held by another process, which in turn is waiting for the first process to release the resource. In general, there is a set of waiting processes, $\{P_1, P_2, \ldots, P_N\}$, such that P_1 is waiting for a resource held by P_2, P_2 is waiting for a resource held by P_3 and so on until P_N is waiting for a resource held by P_1.

---

[15] These four conditions are known as the *Coffman conditions* from their first description in a 1971 article by Edward G. Coffman, Jr.

Most current operating systems do not *prevent* deadlocks (the cost in time and convenience is considered too high for most common situations See 4.2.1.c below). When deadlocks do occur, different operating systems respond to them in different ways. Most of the systems attempt to prevent one of the four Coffman conditions from occurring (most commonly the circular wait condition.)

Major system approaches to the deadlock problem are as follows.

a. *Ignoring deadlock:* In this approach, it is assumed that a deadlock will never occur. This approach was initially used by MINIX and UNIX. This would be appropriate when the time intervals between occurrences of deadlocks are large and the data loss incurred each time is tolerable. In this case, when deadlocks DO occur, human/operator intervention is required (most likely a system reboot.)

b. *Detection*: Under the deadlock detection, deadlocks are allowed to occur. Then the state of the system is examined to detect that a deadlock has in fact occurred and subsequently it is corrected. An algorithm is employed that tracks resource allocation and process states, it rolls back and restarts one or more of the processes in order to remove the detected deadlock. Detecting a deadlock that has already occurred is relatively easy since the resources that each process has locked and/or currently requested are known to the resource scheduler of the operating system. After a deadlock is detected, it can be corrected by using one of the following methods:

   i. *Process termination:* one or more processes involved in the deadlock may be aborted.

      1. One could choose to abort all competing processes involved in the deadlock. This ensures that deadlock is resolved with certainty and speed, but the expense is high since partial computations will be lost.

      2. One could choose to abort one process at a time until the deadlock is resolved. This approach has high overhead because after each abort an algorithm must determine whether the system is still in deadlock. In this case, several factors should be considered while choosing a candidate for termination; factors such as such as priorities and ages of the processes.[1]

   ii. *Resource preemption:* resources allocated to various processes may be successively preempted and allocated to other processes until the deadlock is broken.

c. Prevention: Deadlock prevention works by preventing one of the four Coffman conditions from occurring.

   i. Removing the *mutual exclusion* condition means that no process will have exclusive access to a resource. Algorithms that avoid mutual exclusion are called **non-blocking** synchronization algorithms.

   ii. The *hold and wait* or *resource holding* conditions may be removed by requiring processes to request all the resources they will need before starting up (or before embarking upon a particular set of operations). This advance knowledge is frequently difficult to satisfy and, in any case, is an inefficient use of resources. Another way is to require that a process request resources only when it has none. Thus, first they must release all their currently held resources and then request all the resources they will need. This too is often impractical. It is impractical because resources may be allocated and remain unused for long periods. Also, a process requiring a popular resource may have to wait indefinitely, as such a resource may always be allocated to some other process, resulting in resource starvation. (These algorithms are known as the *all-or-none* *algorithms*.)

iii.   The *no preemption* condition may also be difficult or impossible to avoid as a process has to be able to have a resource for a certain amount of time, or the processing outcome may be inconsistent, or thrashing may occur. However, inability to enforce preemption may interfere with a *priority* algorithm. Preemption of a "locked out" resource generally implies a rollback, and is to be avoided, since it is very costly in overhead. Algorithms that allow preemption include **lock-free** and **wait-free** algorithms and *optimistic concurrency control*. If a process is holding some resources and requests some additional resource(s) that cannot be immediately allocated to it, the condition may be removed by releasing all the currently being held resources of that process.

iv.   The final condition is the *circular wait* condition. Approaches that avoid circular waits include disabling interrupts during critical sections and using a hierarchy to determine a partial ordering of resources. If no obvious hierarchy exists, even the memory address of resources has been used to determine ordering and resources are requested in the increasing order of the enumeration.

4.3   Process Starvation

Starvation is the name given to indefinite postponement of process because it requires some resources before it can run but the resource(s) is/are never allocated to this process, usually because the necessary resource(s) is/are widely used, and the system tends to have numerous higher priority processes making use of it/them.

A common technique to avoid starvation is *aging*, i.e. periodically increasing the priorities of processes that have been blocked for long periods of time. This way, a process that has frequently been denied access to a resource will eventually have its priority raised above that of its competitors and be granted access to the resource.

4.4   Exercises:

4.4.1   In 4.1.2.1   Binary Semaphores, when executing V(S) and the value in S is 0, it is quite possible that there will be multiple processes in the queue of blocked processes. Should all be removed to the ready queue, or only one? What would be the consequences of removing one process and of removing all?

4.4.2   In 4.1.2.2   Counting Semaphores, when executing V(S), it is quite possible that there will be multiple processes in the queue of blocked processes. Should all of them be removed to the ready queue, or should only one be removed? What would be the consequences of removing one process and of removing all?

4.4.3 In the structure of 4.1.3, analyze the consequences of changing the sequences

   a) in function *release*(), placing P(*Available*) immediately after P(*Mutex*) rather than immediately before.

   b) in function *release*(), placing return(resourceArray[i].resource) before V(Mutex) rather than after.

   c) in procedure release(), placing V(Available) immediately before V(Mutex) instead of immediately after.

4.4.4 In setting up the structure of 4.1.3, we assumed that all resources are constant, all either assigned to processes or available for assignment. In a situation such as an airline reservation system, however, resources would be removed from the system (a flight leaves, so no new reservations can be accepted for its seats) and new resources introduced into the system (new flights have their seats made available for booking.). In such a system, then, in addition to assign() and release(), we would also need an addResource() process and removeResource() process.
Describe the variables, semaphores and processes to implement such a system.

4.5 Chapter 4 Questions

4.5.1 True-False

4.5.1.1 All modern operating systems have to deal with the problems of concurrent processes (processes dealing with things that are going on simultaneously.)

4.5.1.2 When concurrent processes can access common memory, many things can go wrong.

4.5.1.3 There is a unique mechanism which has been developed to implement critical regions.

4.5.1.4 In early days of computing, when operating systems were batch systems, it was generally possible for programmers to identify all resources that would be needed by a program. With the advent of interactive systems, however, it has not been feasible to require users to identify in advance the resources that they will be using.

4.5.1.5 Dynamic resource sharing tends to decrease the chance of deadlocks.

4.5.1.6 Detecting a deadlock that has already occurred is easily possible.

4.5.1.7 Most current operating systems cannot prevent deadlocks.

4.5.2 Multiple Choice

4.5.2.1 The common element of all (successful) synchronization schemes is that of a _____ whose execution must be handled as a unit without being interleaved with the execution of others.
   a.   *critical region*
   b.   *hot area*
   c.   *singular section*
   d.   *controlling process*
   e.   none of the above

4.5.2.2 *semaphores:* one of the mechanisms developed to implement critical regions, were invented by _____
   a. Brinch-Hansen
   b. Deitel
   c. Hamming
   d. Tannenbaum
   e. none of the above

4.5.3 Completion

4.5.3.1 All modern operating systems have to deal with the problems of _____ processes (processes dealing with things that are going on simultaneously.)

4.5.3.2 When multiple processes are active at the same time, it is common that some of them will need to _____.

4.5.3.3 Concurrency creates the possibility of _____ and/or starvation.

4.5.3.4 The way that concurrent processes communicate with each other is typically by leaving data/messages in commonly accessible memory locations (_____.)

4.5.3.5 The _____ instruction is an instruction used to write the value 1 to a memory location ("set" the memory location) and return its old value as a single atomic (i.e., non-interruptible) operation.

4.5.3.6 _____ semaphores are typically used to create/implement mutually exclusive critical regions.

4.5.3.7 _____ is a name traditionally assigned to a semaphore used for mutual exclusion.

4.5.3.8 Preventing deadlock by removing the *mutual exclusion* condition means that no process will have exclusive access to a resource. Algorithms that avoid mutual exclusion are called _____ synchronization algorithms.

4.5.3.9 _____ is the name given to indefinite postponement of process because it requires some resources before it can run but the resource(s) is/are never allocated to this process, usually because the necessary resource(s) is/are widely used, and the system tends to have numerous higher priority processes making use of it/them.

5. Policies for Assigning Processor Time

Although most modern computing systems have several processors, the operating systems will typically deal with situations involving more jobs/processes than there are processors, so there will normally be a number of processes waiting to use a processor and there must be some system/policy for choosing a new process when a processor becomes available. There are a number of different policies that have been used, and the policy used in a given system will usually depend on what kind of system it is and what it is used for[16].

Policies for processor selection can be divided into two classes: Preemptive and Non-Preemptive.

> In a *non-preemptive* system, a process, once it is given access to a processor, will be allowed to continue using that processor until it relinquishes control (having finished its task, having come to a point where it needs the results of some I/O operation, or must pause for some other reason.) Only when the process relinquishes control, does the operating system assign the processor to another process.

> In a *preemptive* system, processes are given access to a processor for a fixed (maximum) period of time (a *time slice* aka *quantum.*) The process might well relinquish control before the time slice ends, but if it does not, it will be interrupted. In either case, another process will then be allowed to use the processor.

Very few modern systems are non-preemptive, almost all are preemptive. Systems will differ primarily on length of time slices and priorities for processes in the waiting queue.

Some systems might be designed to prioritize:

> *throughput* (maximize the number of jobs that can be completed)

> *response time* (minimize the time that each user must wait for response)

> *cpu efficiency* (maximize the proportion of time that processor is executing process code[17])

> *job fairness* (each job gets same execution time)

> *system capacity* (maximize number of simultaneous processes/users that the system can/will support)

Systems can also be (and usually are) designed to enforce (other) externally assigned priorities as well as those listed above. These priorities will, of course, vary from one system to another, depending on the function of the system. Most systems will involve a combination of priorities, and will normally be designed to avoid deadlocks and starvation. A priority system aimed at only one of those above would be simplistic and create problems:

---

[16] The policies on a personal computer will be very different from those of a large time sharing system, and those will be different from those used on a supercomputer.

[17] Note: CPU utilization on a device should never reach 100 percent because a device running at 100 percent CPU utilization could be slow to respond to management or system events.

A system prioritizing *throughput* would give highest priority to the shortest jobs and might use relatively long time slices to avoid the overhead involved in unnecessary switching from one process to another. This, however, creates the danger of longer jobs suffering process starvation.

To minimize *response time* a system would prioritize I/O bound (interactive) processes, and would use short time slices to maximize the number of processes working toward the point where they need user interaction. Compute bound processes would obviously suffer from this system.

To maximize *cpu efficiency* a system would use long time slices and prioritize compute bound processes to minimize the frequency of process switching. In such a system I/O bound processes could conceivably suffer starvation and response time would almost certainly suffer.

A system prioritizing *fairness* would use a simple FIFO waiting queue and assign no process priorities. In a busy system with numerous compute bound processes, such a system would result in poor response time.

A system prioritizing *capacity* would prioritize small/short I/O bound processes. Small processes would occupy less RAM, and so more would fit into memory. I/O bound processes spend more time in a paused state, and so put less burden on the processor(s). Larger compute bound processes might suffer starvation.

5.1 Processor Scheduling Algorithms

There are a number of algorithms used by systems for CPU allocation. Some of these algorithms are:

FCFS/FIFO   (First Come First Served/First In First Out) is the simplest scheduling algorithm. It simply queues processes in the order that they arrive. Usually implemented as a non-preemptive system. Once a process has the CPU, it runs to completion. Overhead is minimal, and, assuming all processes complete[18], there would be no starvation. Since would be used on non-preemptive systems, it is only suitable for batch processing, and, as such, was only used on earliest (batch processing) systems.

EDF   (Earliest Deadline First) Processes are placed in a queue ordered by deadlines (times by which they should complete. A form of priority scheduling.) This algorithm is not widely used in a pure form, since behavior is problematic in systems that could become overloaded. (What happens to processes if they do not complete by deadlines?) Deadline time has the effect of aging, so starvation should never be a problem (as long as system never overloads.)

---

[18]   It seems rather naive to assume that no programmer would ever include an infinite loop in his code.

SJN/SJF   (Shortest Job Next, Shortest Job First) Waiting processes are kept in a queue ordered by (estimated) time required to complete execution. When a processor becomes available, the process with shortest execution time is chosen. SJN is another non-preemptive algorithm. The shortest job retains the CPU until it completes (or interrupts.) SRT (below) is a preemptive variant of SJN. Shortest Job Next has advantages of simplicity. It tends to maximize throughput and minimize (average) response time (defined as the average amount of time each process has to wait until its execution begins.) It does, however, have the potential for process starvation. If short processes are continually added, longer processes might never get to run. Again, pure SJN is only suitable for batch systems. It is non-preemptive and requires reliable estimates of execution time (which are generally not available for interactive processes.)

HRRN   (Highest response ratio next) HRRN scheduling is another non-preemptive discipline. It was developed by Brinch Hansen as modification of SJN to mitigate the problem of process starvation. In HRRN, the next job is not that with the shortest estimated run time, but that with the highest *response ratio* defined as
$$responseRatio=(timeWaiting+estimatedRunTime)/estimatedRunTime$$
This means, the jobs that have spent a long time waiting can compete against those estimated to have shorter run times Priorities for longer processes do not increase as fast as those for shorter processes, so shorter processes will always have an advantage, but not an insurmountable advantage. HRRN is a form of priority scheduling (PS) which is designed to implement *aging*.

SRT   (Shortest Remaining Time) This is similar to *shortest job first*. With this strategy the scheduler arranges processes with the shortest estimated processing time remaining to be next in the queue. This requires advanced knowledge (or estimates of) the times required for processes to complete. If a shorter process arrives during another process' execution, the currently running process is interrupted, and its estimated time to complete would be updated, and the interrupted process would be returned to the waiting queue. Of course all of this adds to the system overhead. The scheduler must also place each incoming process into a specific place in the queue, and this creates even more overhead. The SRT algorithm is designed for maximum throughput in most scenarios, but, because of increased overhead, might, in fact, be slower than SJN. Waiting time and response time increase as the process's computational requirements increase. Since turnaround time is based on waiting time plus processing time, longer processes are significantly affected by this. Starvation is possible in SRT, especially in a busy system with many small processes.

RR   (Round Robin[xv]) RR is a preemptive scheduling system. The scheduler assigns a fixed time unit per process, and cycles through them. If a process completes within a time-slice it gets terminated otherwise it will be rescheduled after all other processes have had their opportunity. RR scheduling involves

Round Robin Scheduling

considerable overhead (especially if the system uses a short time unit.) In practice, it results in throughput between that of FCFS and SJF. Shorter jobs are completed faster than in FCFS and longer processes are completed faster than in SJF. It generally has good average response time, since waiting times depend on number of processes, and not lengths of other processes. Starvation will never occur, since no special priority is given to any process.

PS (Priority Scheduling) Non-preemptive priority scheduling is one of the most common scheduling systems in batch systems. It gives preferential treatment to some jobs at the cost of other (presumably less important) ones. (SJF and HRRN are examples of PS scheduling.) The programs with highest priorities are processed first and are not interrupted until they complete or pause themselves. Priorities can be assigned based on many different characteristics (who the user is, how much memory required, what peripheral devices required, total run time, how long it has been waiting i.e. *aging*, and many others.)

FPPS   (Fixed-Priority Preemptive Scheduling) is a scheduling system commonly used in real-time systems. With fixed priority preemptive scheduling, the scheduler ensures that at any given time, the processor executes the highest priority task of all those tasks that are currently ready to execute. The process is given a time slice (quantum) and, when the process self-interrupts, or completes, or finishes its time slice, the preemptive scheduler has the option of once again identifying the highest priority task from among those ready to execute. This scheduling system has the advantage of making sure no task hogs the processor for any time longer than the time slice. However, this scheduling scheme is vulnerable to process or thread lockout: since priority is given to higher-priority tasks, the lower-priority tasks could wait an indefinite amount of time. One common method of arbitrating this situation is aging, which gradually increments the priority of waiting processes and threads, ensuring that they will all eventually execute. Most real-time operating systems (RTOS's) have preemptive schedulers.

CFS   (Completely Fair Scheduler) is a process scheduler which was merged into the 2.6.23 (October 2007) release of the Linux kernel[xvi] and is the default scheduler. It handles CPU resource allocation for executing processes and aims to maximize overall CPU utilization while also maximizing interactive performance. Like the old O(1) scheduler, CFS uses a concept called "sleeper fairness",

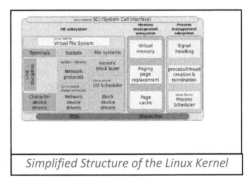

Simplified Structure of the Linux Kernel

which considers sleeping or waiting tasks equivalent to those on the run queue. This means that interactive tasks which spend most of their time waiting for user input or other events get a comparable share of CPU time when they need it.

Multiple Level Queues[xvii]   When processes can be divided into a few distinct categories, then multiple separate queues can be established. Different scheduling algorithms can also be implemented on the different queues if different algorithms are appropriate for the different types of jobs.

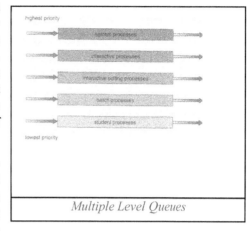

Multiple Level Queues

One example could be foreground-interactive processes and background-batch processes. These two types of processes have different response-time requirements and so will have different scheduling needs. Another common subdivision is that of I/O bound and compute bound processes.

When using multiple queues, scheduling must also be done between the queues, that is scheduling one queue to get time relative to other queues. Two common options are:

strict priority (no job in a lower priority queue runs until all higher priority queues are empty)

round-robin (each queue gets a time slice in turn. (Some systems assign different time slice sizes for processes from different queues.)

Note that under this algorithm, it is assumed that jobs do not move from one queue to another - Once they are assigned a queue, that is their queue until they finish.

Multilevel Feedback-Queue Scheduling[xviii]   Multilevel feedback queue scheduling is similar to the ordinary multilevel queue scheduling described above, except that jobs may be moved from one queue to another for a variety of reasons:

Multilevel Feedback Queue Scheduling

o   If the characteristics of a job change (such as between CPU-intensive and I/O intensive) then it may be appropriate to switch a job from one queue to another.

o   Aging can also be incorporated, so that a job that has waited for a long time can get bumped up into a higher priority queue.

Multilevel feedback queue scheduling is the more flexible than strict multilevel queue scheduling because it can be tuned for any situation. It is, however, much more complex to implement because of all the adjustable parameters.

Some of the parameters which define one of these systems include:

o The number of queues.
o The scheduling algorithm for each queue.
o The methods used to upgrade or demote processes from one queue to another. (Which may not be the same for all queues)
o The method used to determine which queue a process enters initially.

5.2 Processor Affinity[xix]

When designing a scheduling algorithm for a multiprocessor system, there is the additional problem of identifying which processor to use for a given process. Should some of the processes have "preferred" processors, or should a process, when its turn comes in the waiting queue, simply be assigned to the first processor that becomes available.

One of the factors that complicates this decision is cache memory. Individual processors typically have their own cache memory which speeds up repeated accesses to the same memory locations. If a process were to switch from one processor to another each time it got a time slice, the data in the cache (for that process) would have to be invalidated and re-loaded from main memory, and this would eliminate much of the benefit of the cache.

Usually then, systems attempt to keep assigning processes to the same processor, using techniques called *processor affinity.*

> *Soft affinity* occurs when the system *attempts* to keep processes on the same processor but makes no guarantees.

> *Hard affinity,* on the other hand, describes a system in which a process specifies that it is not to be moved between processors. Linux supports *hard affinity*. (as do some other OS's.)

Main memory architecture can also affect process affinity, if particular CPUs have faster access to memory on the same chip or board than to other memory loaded elsewhere. (*Non-Uniform Memory Access*, or NUMA.) If a process has an affinity for a particular CPU, then it should preferentially be assigned memory storage in "local" fast access areas.

60

5.2.1 Virtualization and Scheduling

Virtualization adds another layer of complexity for scheduling. Typically, there would be one host operating system operating on "real" processor(s) and a number of "guest" operating systems executing on virtual processors. The Host OS creates some number of virtual processors and presents them to the guest operating systems as if they were real processors. The guest OSes don't "realize" that they are executing on virtual processors and make scheduling decisions on the assumption that they are executing on real processors. As a result, real-time performance (and especially interactive performances) can be severely compromised on guest systems.

5.3 Exercises

5.3.1 There are a number of different policies that have been used, and the policy chosen for a given system will usually depend on what kind of system it is and what it is used for. What are some of the different kinds of things a system might be used for, and how might they affect the design of the operating systems used for them?

5.3.2 It has been argued that, since reassigning control from one process to another necessarily requires a certain amount of computer time (overhead), non-preemptive systems are inherently more efficient than preemptive systems. How valid is this argument?

5.4 Questions

5.4.1 True-False

5.4.1.1 Since most modern computing systems have several processors, it is rare for the operating systems to have to deal with situations involving more jobs/processes than there are processors.

5.4.1.2 Very few modern systems are non-preemptive, almost all are preemptive

5.4.1.3 A device running at 100 percent CPU utilization would be very quick to respond to management or system events.

5.4.1.4 One of the primary advantages of RR scheduling is that it involves relatively little overhead.

5.4.2 Multiple Choice

5.4.2.1 To _____ a system would prioritize I/O bound (interactive) processes, and use short time slices to maximize the number of processes working toward the point where they need user interaction. Compute bound processes would obviously suffer from this system
  a. minimize *response time*
  b. maximize *cpu efficiency*
  c. prioritize *fairness*
  d. prioritize *capacity*
  e. none of the above

5.4.2.2   To _____ a system would use a simple fifo waiting queue and assign no process priorities.
  a.   minimize *response time*
  b.   maximize *cpu efficiency*
  c.   prioritize *fairness*
  d.   prioritize *capacity*
  e.   none of the above

5.4.2.3   There are a number of algorithms used by systems for CPU allocation. One of these _____ is the simplest, but was only used on the earliest batch processing systems
  a.   FIFO
  b.   SJF
  c.   HRRN
  d.   FPPS
  e.   none of the above

5.4.2.4   There are a number of algorithms used by systems for CPU allocation. One of these _____ is the default scheduler for the Linux kernel
  a.   FIFO
  b.   SJF
  c.   HRRN
  d.   FPPS
  e.   none of the above

5.4.2.5   There are a number of algorithms used by systems for CPU allocation. One of these _____ places processes in a queue ordered by estimated processing time remaining
  a.   EDF
  b.   SRT
  c.   RR
  d.   PS
  e.   none of the above

5.4.3   Completion

5.4.3.1   In a(n) _____ system, a process, once it is given access to a processor, will be allowed to continue using that processor until it relinquishes control.

5.4.3.2   A system is said to prioritize _____ if it is designed to maximize the number of jobs that can be completed.

5.4.3.3   PS is one of the most common scheduling systems in _____ systems.

5.4.3.4   _____ *affinity* occurs when the system attempts to keep processes on the same processor but makes no guarantees.

6. Memory Management

Recall (from chapter 1) external storage is much cheaper than RAM, so it seems obvious that more processes can be accommodated (on a system of the same price) if suspended programs would be stored on disk, rather than occupying relatively expensive RAM, (at least stored on disk until they are ready to resume execution.) Systems, then, have been developed that use disk space as an extension of primary storage in this way. (Using secondary storage as *virtual* memory. Description starting in section 6.1) Much of the effectiveness of such *virtual memory systems* can be attributed to the "Principle of Locality" (See section 1.2.7.1)

Newer technologies for higher speed RAM have been developed, but this RAM is more expensive, requires more power and produces more heat than does the more commonly used (and slower) RAM. Systems have been developed using small sections (caches) of the high speed RAM and copying the contents of standard RAM into the caches to make use of the high speed technology while doing computation. The effective use of cache memory systems also depends on the "Principle of Locality". The description of cache memory system starts in section 6.4.

As mentioned in section 1.2.9, many programs do a great deal of I/O to and from secondary storage (disk), frequently saving data and/or retrieving data. The progress of such programs is very much impeded by the relatively slow disk access. In order to speed the progress of these I/O bound programs *virtual disk* systems similar to memory cache systems have been designed that retain in RAM copies of recently referenced sections of disk where they can be referenced more quickly. (See section 6.8.)

A number of functions and procedures (often provided in *libraries*) are widely used by numerous programs, possibly programs/processes executing simultaneously. Since it is not desirable that each instance of each process have its own copy of a common subprogram, operating systems have been designed to support *dynamic linking* providing access to a single copy of a subprogram by multiple instances of multiple processes. (See section 6.6 for more about dynamic linking.)

6.1 Virtual Memory Systems

Virtual memory systems have been developed that can identify sections of RAM that are unlikely to be referenced in the immediate future and copy the contents of these sections to disk, allowing those areas of RAM to be used for data or code that IS likely to be utilized in the near future. The sections of memory copied to disk might include entire programs/processes that are paused waiting on some event, but could also include subsections of a relatively large program even while that program executes. A large program might be divided into sections, and while it is executing, using commands and data in one section, other sections of the program might not be in use and could be swapped out to disk.

Keeping track of what has been copied to disk (and where it is on disk) clearly adds to the complexity of the operating systems. Now they are also required to manage virtual memory systems: they must identify which programs and/or program segments will (probably) not be referenced immediately; they must keep track of where on disk the swapped out pages/segments are stored; they must be able to retrieve them; they must determine where in RAM to copy them after retrieval.

As stated above, virtual memory systems can be effective in largely because of the "Principle of Locality". This principle states that memory references by the processor tend to cluster.

If, for a reasonable period of time, none of the cells in a particular section of memory have been referenced, then it is likely that the next several memory references will continue to be to cells in different sections of memory, and so, if the "*none reference*" section were to be swapped out, the system performance would not be affected (at least for a while.)

Disk access involves two steps: The movement of an arm to place a read/write head over the correct track (the time that it takes to do this is called the seek time for the access) and then the disk must rotate until the head aligns with the desired sector[19] with the head (the time that it takes to do this is called the *rotational latency* of the access.)
Seek time is typically much longer than rotational latency.

Consequently, data transfer to and from a disk is much more efficient if sections of data that will be referenced together are stored on the same disk track, or at least on tracks very close together. With this configuration, arm movement is minimized and less time will be needed to read or write related information.

This observation provided the motivation for the development of *paging* systems.

Virtual memory systems are subject to **thrashing**, which occurs when the computer's virtual memory resources become saturated, leading to a constant state of exchanging data in memory for data on disk, to the exclusion of most application-level processing. Virtual memory operating systems must be carefully designed to avoid this problem.

6.2   Paging Memory Systems:

As we have seen, it had become necessary (or at least highly desirable) to design a system that would support the efficient (re)positioning of programs and data for transfers between RAM and secondary storage, and, as we will see shortly, between RAM and cache memory as well.

The system that has been developed is called *paging*.

---

[19]   A *sector* is the basic unit of data storage on a hard disk. The term "sector refers to a pie shaped angular section of a circle, bounded on two sides by radii and the third by the perimeter of the circle. A hard disk is comprised of a group of predefined sectors that form a circle. That circle of predefined sectors is

defined as a single track.
A group of concentric circles (tracks) define a single surface of a disks platter.
Early hard disks had just a single one-sided platter, while today's hard disks are comprised of several platters with tracks on both sides, all of which comprise the entire hard disk capacity. Early hard disks had the same number of sectors per track location, and in fact, the number of sectors in each track were fairly standard between models. Today's advances in drive technology, however, have allowed the number of sectors per track (SPT) to vary significantly.
(www.dewassoc.com/kbase/hard_drives/hard_disk_sector_structures.htm)

The OS has five principal storage management responsibilities:

> process isolation;
> allocation and management;
> modular programming support;
> protection and access control
> long-term storage,

and *paging* systems (of necessity) provide support for all of these.

The term ***Paging*** is used to describe a system in which processes are made up of a number of fixed size blocks, called pages. In a paging system, a program references a word by means of a *virtual address*, which is implemented as a *page number* and an *offset* within the page. Each page can be located anywhere in main memory. Paging provides a system for a dynamic mapping between the virtual addresses used in the program and real (or physical) addresses in main memory. Such a system is necessary to support a virtual memory system. In order to minimize access times, the contents of a page will normally be stored in the same disk sector or (less frequently) in adjacent disk sectors. Thus, page sizes tend to be dictated by sector sizes on attached hard disks.

6.2.1 Virtual Memory Addressing[xx]

In a system using virtual memory (with paging) processes and data sets will be organized in files, each occupying one or more pages on secondary storage. (Some pages will have copies in primary storage, and some will not. The CPU, of course, can only deal directly with locations in primary storage.)

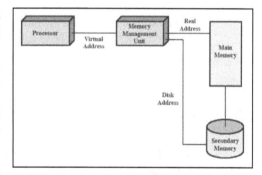

In such a system, when a CPU references an entity, it identifies the page of the entity, and its location on the page (as an offset from the beginning of the page.) The MMU will have a table of the pages, and records of whether they have copies in RAM (and, if so, where in RAM they are located.) When the processor references an address on a page, the MMU uses its table to determine whether that page is in RAM. If it is in RAM, the MMU directs the reference to the appropriate RAM address. If the page with the referenced location is not in RAM, the MMU pauses the CPU process and initiates the process of copying the page with the referenced location into RAM.

6.2.2 Virtual Memory with Paging[xxi]

When a process begins execution in a virtual memory system implemented by paging, only the page containing its initial section is called into memory. The principle of locality suggests that the first few operations will reference memory locations in that page. If, at some point, a location on another page is referenced, then the process will pause, the 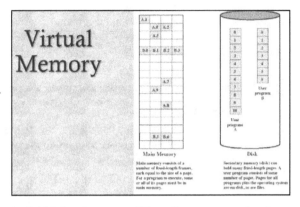 system will find, or create space in RAM for that page. When the new page has been loaded, the process can continue executing.

If there are many processes executing, it is likely that all available memory would be in use and, when a memory reference is made to a location not currently in RAM, there would be no unallocated RAM locations. In such a case the contents of some RAM page must be copied to disk and then the page with the referenced address can be copied from disk into the RAM page whose contents were just saved. This system requires that there be some kind of policy for selecting pages that are to be copied to disk. Often such a system involves an algorithm for predicting which pages would be unlikely be referenced in the immediate future.

There are a number of possible strategies for choosing a page to swap out to disk. Among these strategies are:

FIFO (First In First Out) The page to be replaced would be the one that has been in RAM the longest. This strategy is relatively easy to implement, and it seems intuitive that a page that has been in RAM for the longest might be less likely to be referenced in the near future than others that were copied into RAM more recently. Unfortunately, in many systems this algorithm has been seen to target popular library functions used by many processes. Commonly used functions will tend to get referenced (and copied into RAM) early (and often.) When swapped out, these pages will be referenced, and copied back into RAM almost immediately. Although FIFO is a poor predictor of future inactivity, it is one of the simplest strategies to implement. It is a low-overhead algorithm that requires little bookkeeping on the part of the operating system. The idea is obvious from the name – the operating system keeps track of all the pages in memory in a queue, with the most recent arrival at the back, and the oldest arrival in front. When a page needs to be replaced, the page at the front of the queue (the oldest page) is selected. While FIFO is cheap and intuitive, it performs poorly in practical application. Thus, it is rarely used in its unmodified form. The FIFO page replacement algorithm is used by the VAX/VMS operating system, but with some modifications. Partial second chance (see below) is one of these modifications

Second-chance: A modified form of the FIFO page replacement algorithm, known as the *Second-chance* page replacement algorithm, fares relatively better than FIFO, and with little additional cost. Second-chance works by looking at the front of the queue as FIFO does, but instead of immediately paging out that page, it checks to see if its *referenced bit*[20] is set. If it is not set, the page is swapped out. Otherwise, the referenced bit is cleared, the page is inserted at the back of the queue (as if it were a new page) and this process is repeated. This can also be thought of as a circular queue. If all the pages have their referenced bit set, on the second encounter of the first page in the list, that page will be swapped out, as it now has its referenced bit cleared. If all the pages have their reference bit cleared, then Second-chance algorithm degenerates into pure FIFO. As its name suggests, Second-chance gives every page a "second-chance" – an old page that has been referenced is probably in use and should not be swapped out instead of a new page that has not been referenced.

Clock is a more efficient version of FIFO than Second-chance because pages don't have to be constantly pushed to the back of the list, but it performs the same general function as Second-Chance. The clock algorithm keeps a circular list of pages in memory, with the "hand" (iterator) pointing to the last examined page frame in the list. When a page fault occurs and no empty frames exist, then the referenced bit (R) is inspected at the hand's location. If R is 0, the new page is put in place of the page the "hand" points to. Otherwise, the R bit is cleared, then the clock hand is incremented and the process is repeated until a page is replaced. If all the pages have their reference bit cleared, then Clock algorithm degenerates into pure FIFO.

LRU (Least Recently Used) This strategy replaces the page that has gone the longest without a reference. According to the principle of locality, this should give the best performance. Unfortunately, LRU is relatively difficult to implement efficiently. It tends to require more processing and storage overhead than do other techniques. The LRU page replacement algorithm, although similar in name to NRU (described below), differs in the fact that LRU keeps track of page usage over a short period of time, while NRU just looks at the usage in the last clock interval. LRU works on the idea that pages that have been most heavily used in the past few instructions are most likely to be used heavily in the next few instructions too. While LRU can provide near-optimal performance in theory, it is rather expensive to implement in practice. There are a few implementation methods for this algorithm that try to reduce the cost yet keep as much of the performance as possible.

---

[20] When a page is referenced, a *referenced bit* is set for that page, marking it as referenced. Similarly, when a page is modified (written to), a modified bit is set. The setting of the bits is usually done by the hardware, although it is possible to do so on the software level.
At a certain fixed time interval, a timer interrupt triggers and clears the referenced bit of all the pages, so only pages referenced within the current timer interval are marked with a referenced bit.

The most expensive method is the *linked list* method, which uses a linked list containing all the pages in memory. At the back of this list is the least recently used page, and at the front is the most recently used page. The cost of this implementation lies in the fact that items in the list will have to be moved with every memory reference, which is a very time-consuming process.

Another method that requires hardware support is as follows: suppose the hardware has a 64-bit counter that is incremented at every instruction. Whenever a page is accessed, it acquires the value equal to the counter at the time of page access. Whenever a page needs to be replaced, the operating system selects the page with the lowest counter and swaps it out. With present hardware, this is not feasible because the OS would need to examine the counter for every page in memory.

Because of implementation costs, one may consider algorithms that are similar to LRU, but which offer cheaper implementations. One important advantage of the LRU algorithm is that it is amenable to full statistical analysis. It has been proven, for example, that LRU can never result in more than N-times more page faults than an optimum algorithm, where N is proportional to the number of pages in the managed pool.

On the other hand, LRU's weakness is that its performance tends to degenerate under many quite common reference patterns.

For example, if there are N pages in the LRU pool, an application executing a loop over array of N + 1 pages will cause a page fault on each and every access. As loops over large arrays are common, much effort has been put into modifying LRU to work better in such situations. Many of the proposed LRU modifications try to detect looping reference patterns and to switch into a more suitable replacement algorithm, like Most Recently Used (MRU).

LFU (Least Frequently Used) This strategy selects the page that has been accessed least frequently. LFU can be implemented more efficiently (with less overhead) than LRU, but has a tendency to target the most recently loaded pages before they have an opportunity to have established themselves as being used frequently.

NRU (Not Recently Used) The not recently used (NRU) page replacement algorithm is an algorithm that favors keeping pages in memory that have been recently used. NRU uses the following technique: when a page is referenced, a *referenced* bit is set for that page, marking it as having been referenced. If a page is modified (written to), a *modified* bit is set. The setting of the bits is usually done by the hardware, although it is possible to do so on the software level as well. At fixed intervals a timer interrupt triggers and clears all of the *referenced* bits (but not the *modified* bits.) Thus, at any time only pages referenced recently (within the current timer interval) are marked with a set *referenced* bit. When a page needs to be replaced, the operating system first searches for a page with both the *referenced* bit and the *modified* bit clear.

With a clear *referenced* bit, the principle of locality suggests that information on the page is unlikely to be referenced soon and with a clear *modified* bit, the information on the page is the same as that on disk, so it does not need to be written to disk before the page is overwritten.

If there are no pages with both bits clear, then the system searches for a page with just the *referenced* bit clear. The information on this page will be copied to disk, and then the page will be overwritten.

Again, with a clear *referenced* bit, it is unlikely that the page will be revisited soon.

If there are no pages with clear *referenced* bit, then the system searches for a page with clear *modified* bit.

In this case, although the page is likely to be revisited relatively soon, at least recycling it will not involve time copying content to disk.

Finally, if all pages have both bits set, then a page is chosen at random, its content copied to disk and then it is overwritten with the new data.

NFU (Not frequently used) The not frequently used page replacement algorithm requires a counter, and every page has one counter of its own which is initially set to 0. At each clock interval, all pages that have been referenced within that interval will have their counter incremented by 1. In effect, the counters keep track of how frequently a page has been used. Thus, the page with the lowest counter can be swapped out when necessary. The main problem with NFU is that it keeps track of the frequency of use without regard to the time span of use. Thus, in a multi-pass compiler, pages which were heavily used during the first pass, but are not needed in the second pass will be favored over pages which are comparably lightly used in the second pass, as they have higher frequency counters. This results in poor performance. Other common scenarios also exist where NFU will perform similarly One such is an OS boot-up.

Aging: The aging algorithm is a descendant of the NFU algorithm, with modifications to make it aware of the time span of use. Instead of just incrementing the counters of pages referenced, putting equal emphasis on page references regardless of the time, the reference counter on a page is first shifted right (divided by 2), before adding the referenced bit to the left of that binary number. Page references closer to the current time have more impact than earlier page references. This ensures that pages referenced more recently, even though less frequently, will have higher priority over pages frequently referenced in the past. Of course, when a page needs to be swapped out, the page with the lowest counter will be chosen.

Random Although not widely used, the strategy of simply choosing a page at random actually works almost as well as most others and has the advantage of being easy to implement and with virtually no overhead. Random replacement algorithm replaces a random page in memory. This eliminates the overhead cost of tracking page references. Usually it fares better than FIFO, and for looping memory references it is better than LRU, although generally LRU performs better in practice. OS/390 uses global LRU approximation and falls back to random replacement when LRU performance degenerates, and the Intel i860 processor used a random replacement.

6.2.3 Developments Concerning Page Replacement Algorithms

Page replacement algorithms were a hot topic of research and debate in the 1960s and 1970s. That mostly ended with the development of sophisticated LRU (least recently used) approximations and working set algorithms. Since then, though, some basic assumptions made by the traditional page replacement algorithms were invalidated, and that resulted in a revival of research.

In particular, the following trends in the behavior of underlying hardware and user-level software have affected the performance of page replacement algorithms:

Size of primary storage has increased by multiple orders of magnitude. With several gigabytes of primary memory, algorithms that require a periodic check of every memory frame are becoming less and less practical.

Locality of reference has weakened for user software. This is mostly attributed to the spread of object-oriented programming techniques that tend to use large numbers of small functions and the greater use of more sophisticated data structures like trees and hash tables that tend to result in chaotic memory reference patterns.

In addition, differences in operating system kernel architectures have changed requirements for page replacement algorithms. In particular, most modern OS kernels have unified virtual memory and file system caches, and this requires the page replacement algorithm to select a page from among the pages of both user program virtual address spaces and cached files. The latter pages have specific properties. For example, they can be locked, or can have write ordering requirements imposed. Moreover, as the goal of page replacement is to minimize total time waiting for memory, it has to take into account memory requirements imposed by other kernel sub-systems that allocate memory. As a result, page replacement in modern kernels (Linux, FreeBSD, and Solaris) tends to work at the level of a general purpose kernel memory allocator, rather than at the higher level of a virtual memory subsystem.

6.3 Memory Segmentation

Memory segmentation is the division of a computer's primary memory into **segments** or **sections**. Unlike pages, segments are not generally of uniform sizes, and are generally controlled by programmers, rather than the operating system.

In a computer system using segmentation, a reference to a memory location includes a value that identifies a segment and another value specifying the offset (memory location) within that segment. Segments (or sections) are also used in object files of compiled programs when they are linked together into a program image which then can be loaded into memory.

Segments usually correspond to natural divisions of a program such as individual routines or data tables, so segmentation is generally more visible to the programmer than paging alone. Different segments may be created for different program modules, or for different classes of memory usage such as code and data segments. Certain segments may be shared between programs.

In a system using segmentation, computer memory addresses consist of a segment id and an offset within the segment. The MMU is responsible for translating the segment and offset into a physical address, and for performing checks to make sure the translation can be done and that the reference to that segment and offset is permitted.

Each segment has a length and will normally have a set of permissions (for example, *read*, *write*, *execute*) associated with it. A process would only be allowed to make a reference into a segment if the type of reference is allowed by the permissions, and if the offset within the segment is within the range specified by the length of the segment. Otherwise, a hardware exception, such as a segmentation fault, would be raised.

Segments may also be used to implement virtual memory. In this case, the MMU would have a segment table (similar to the page table described above[21].) Each segment entry would have an associated flag indicating whether it is present in main memory or not. If a segment is accessed that is not present in main memory, an exception would be raised, and the operating system would read the segment into memory from secondary storage.

Segmentation has been implemented in several different ways on different hardware, with or without paging.

6.3.1   Intel x86 Memory Segmentation

Intel x86 memory segmentation does not fit either of the models just described. The memory segmentation used by early x86 processors, beginning with the Intel 8086, does not provide any protection. Any program running on these processors can access any segment with no restrictions. A segment is only identified by its starting location; there is no length checking, and this, obviously, creates serious security issues. Segmentation in the Intel 80286 and later versions of the 80x86 architecture, does provide length checking protection.

6.3.2   Virtual Memory with Segmentation

Virtual memory with segmentation functions much the same was as virtual memory with paging. Process code and data are subdivided into *segments* which can be stored on disk, loaded individually into RAM as needed, and copied back to secondary storage when it would seem they would not be referenced soon. Thus, segments in a virtual memory system with segments, are treated much as pages are treated in a paging virtual memory system.

Since segments tend to correspond to logical subdivisions in a program rather than physical subdivisions in data storage, there will be less reading and writing back and forth in a segmented virtual memory system than in a paging system. (Often, most of the code will be compiled into the same segment, and thus all coding references will generally be to commands in the same segment, all of which would be loaded into RAM together. Similarly, related data would tend to be contained in the same segment and would also

---

[21]   Paging can, in fact, be combined with segmentation.

all loaded together.) Segmentation systems, then, will be much less subject to thrashing than will paging systems.

On the other hand, because segments are not of uniform size, virtual memory systems using segmentation are subject to fragmentation of their primary storage systems. There are techniques for avoiding, or reducing such fragmentation, but these all add significantly to the MMU overhead.

Fragmentation of RAM

6.4 Cache Memory

The principle of locality can be applied in the other direction as well.

New technology was being developed that permitted the creation of RAM that supported faster and faster memory references. This new faster RAM, however, was also much more expensive. It was not (and still is not) cost effective to build computers in which all of the RAM used the high speed technology. It was, however, (and is) possible to include a relatively small amount of high speed RAM (called a cache.)

If a CPU references a cell in a given section of RAM, then it is likely that the next few memory references will also be to cells in that same section. This observation motivated the development of systems that use small segments of high speed RAM (caches.) The contents of blocks of RAM containing sections likely to be referenced soon are copied into these caches.

These cache systems permit the effective use of high speed but expensive forms of RAM. If a CPU references a cell in a given section of cache, then it is likely that the next few memory references will also be to cells in that same section. If the processor references a location in normal RAM, the section of memory containing that cell would be copied into the cache, and, by the principle of locality, the next several memory references would probably be made using the high speed RAM in the cache. In this way, although only using only a small amount of memory with high speed technology, most of the CPU operations would be executed using that high speed memory.

Of course, in systems with cache memory, the operating system has the additional responsibility of keeping track of which memory sections are duplicated in cache, which sections have been referenced recently, and which cache cells have had their contents modified (and must therefore be copied back to regular RAM before being replaced by more recently accessed memory sections.)

Just as with virtual memory, cache memory systems are subject to thrashing, and effective replacement strategies are critical to their success.

6.4.1 Blocks

Cache memory uses a technique similar to paging, but caches tend to be rather smaller than pages. The cache is divided into standard sized sections, called *blocks*.

When a process references an address, the system checks to see if that address is already represented in cache. If it is not, the system will try to find an empty block in cache, and if there is, a section RAM the size of a block and containing the referenced address will be copied into the unused block in cache. If there is no unused block, the system will choose one of the blocks to overwrite. The contents of a section RAM the size of a block and containing the referenced address will be copied into the selected block in cache. Once it is determined that the referenced address is represented in cache, the process resumes execution, using the contents of words stored in cache and not those in RAM.

As with virtual memory, if a block must be overwritten, there are several algorithms used to choose which one to overwrite.

6.4.2 Values in Cache that have been Modified

One of the factors that must be taken into consideration when choosing a block to remove from cache is whether the contents of the block have been modified. When cache data has been modified, it should be copied back to RAM before the block is overwritten, because if not, information will be lost. Clearly the process of copying the contents of a cache block to RAM and then copying new data into the block takes more time than simply copying the new data into the block.

Further, if data in a cache block has been modified, there exists the possibility that another process might attempt to reference the same data (whose cache version has been modified.) There are three ways this could play out:

The system might keep a record of which blocks are in cache and allow the second process also to reference the copy of data in cache. This system requires extra (high speed) memory for these records, and each memory reference by the processor must be processed using this record. This would clearly not be an option for multiprocessor systems in which processors do not all share all of their caches. It also raises all of the problems involved in simultaneous access (see Chapter 4.)

The system might require that any block with modified data be copied back to RAM as soon as it is modified, so that the information in cache is always a faithful representation of the corresponding block in RAM. This technique will require many more write operations from cache to RAM than the alternatives, and reduces the effectiveness of the use of cache, especially for processes that make frequent modifications to contents of memory cells.

The system might permit the second process to access the data as it appears in RAM (which in this scenario, would not be the "correct" information as calculated by the first process. i.e. would be "dirty" data)

6.4.3 Cache Replacement Algorithms

cache algorithms (also frequently called cache replacement algorithms or cache replacement *policies*) are algorithms that a program or a hardware-maintained structure can use to manage a cache of information stored on the computer. When the cache is full, the algorithm must choose which items to discard to make room for the new ones.

There are two primary measures used for the management of a cache: The *latency*, and the *hit rate*. There are also a number of secondary factors affecting cache performance.

Hit Rate: The "hit rate" (or "hit ratio") of a cache describes how often a searched-for item is actually found in the cache. More efficient replacement policies keep track of more usage information in order to improve the hit rate (for a given cache size) Hit rate measurements are typically performed on benchmark applications, since the actual hit ratio varies widely from one application to another. In particular, video and audio streaming applications often have a hit ratio close to zero, because each bit of data in the stream is read once for the first time (a compulsory miss), used, and then never re-read or written again. Even worse, many cache algorithms (in particular, LRU) allow this streaming data to fill the cache, pushing information that will be used again soon out of the cache (cache pollution).

Latency: The "latency" of a cache describes how long after requesting a desired item the cache can return that item (when there is a hit). Faster replacement strategies typically keep track of less usage information—or, in the case of direct-mapped cache, no information—to reduce the amount of time required to update that information.

Each replacement strategy is a compromise between hit rate and latency.

Other factors that might be considered include:

- Items with different cost: keep items that are expensive to obtain, e.g. those that take a long time to get.

- Items taking up more cache: If items have different sizes, the cache may want to discard a large item to provide space to store several smaller ones.

- Items that expire with time: Some caches keep information that expires (e.g. a news cache, a DNS cache, or a web browser cache). The computer may discard items because they are expired. Depending on the size of the cache no further caching algorithm to discard items may be necessary.

Replacement policies for cache are, for the most part, very similar to those for virtual memory:

FIFO (First in first out) Using this algorithm the cache behaves in the same way as a FIFO queue. The cache evicts the first block accessed first without any regard to how often or how many times it was accessed before. FIFO is simple to implement and has very low overhead.

LRU (Least recently used) Discards the least recently used items first. This algorithm requires keeping track of what was used and when. This is expensive if one wants to make sure the algorithm *always* discards the least recently used item. General implementations of this technique require keeping "age bits" for cache-lines and track the "Least Recently Used" cache-line based on age-bits. In such an implementation, every time a cache-line is used, the age of all other cache-lines changes.

PLRU (Pseudo LRU) For larger caches, the implementation cost of LRU becomes prohibitive. In many CPU caches, a scheme that usually discards one of the less recently used items is sufficient, and so, many CPU designers choose a PLRU algorithm which only needs one bit per cache item to work. PLRU typically has a slightly worse miss ratio, has a slightly better latency, uses slightly less power than LRU and has lower overhead compared to LRU.

TLRU (Time aware least recently used) The Time aware Least Recently Used is a variant of LRU designed for the situation where the stored contents in cache have a valid life time. The algorithm is suitable in some network cache applications, and especially for distributed networks.

MRU (Most recently used) In contrast to LRU, discards the *most* recently used items first. It has been shown[22] that when a file is being repeatedly scanned in a looping sequential pattern, MRU is the best replacement algorithm." MRU algorithms are, of course, most useful in situations where the older an item is, the more likely it is to be accessed.

RR (Random replacement) Randomly selects a candidate item and discards it to make space when necessary. This algorithm does not require keeping any information about the access history. For its simplicity, it has been used in ARM (Ashton Raggatt MacDougall) processors.

LFU (Least-frequently used) Counts how often an item is needed. Those that are used least often are discarded first. This works very similar to LRU except that instead of storing the value of how recently a block was accessed, we store the value of how many times it was accessed.

LFUDA (LFU with Dynamic Aging) LFUDA uses dynamic aging to accommodate shifts in the set of popular objects. It adds a cache age factor to the reference count when a new object is added to the cache or when an existing object is re-referenced. LFUDA increments the cache ages when removing blocks. If an object was frequently accessed in the past and now it becomes unpopular, the newly or less popular objects would be allowed to replace it.

---

[22] By Chou and DeWitt in findings presented at the 11th VLDB conference

6.4.4 Cache Memory Associativity[xxii]

The replacement policy decides where in the cache a copy of a particular entry of main memory will go. If the replacement policy is free to choose any entry in the cache to hold the copy, the cache is called *fully associative*. At the other extreme, if each entry in main memory can go in just one place in the cache, the cache is *direct mapped*. Many caches implement a

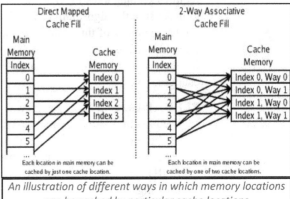

An illustration of different ways in which memory locations can be cached by particular cache locations

compromise in which each entry in main memory can go to any one of N places in the cache, and are described as N-way set associative. For example, the level-1 data cache in an AMD (Advanced Micro Devices) Athlon processor is two-way set associative, which means that any particular location in main memory can be cached in either of two locations in the level-1 data cache.

Choosing the right value of associativity involves a trade-off. If there are ten places to which the replacement policy could have mapped a memory location, then to check if that location is in the cache, ten cache entries must be searched. Checking more places takes more power and chip area, and potentially more time. On the other hand, caches with more associativity suffer fewer misses so that the CPU wastes less time reading from the slow main memory. The general guideline is that doubling the associativity, from direct mapped to two-way, or from two-way to four-way, has about the same effect on raising the hit rate as doubling the cache size. However, increasing associativity more than four does not improve hit rate as much, and, when done, it is generally done for other reasons.

In order of worse hit rate but simple implementation to better hit rate but more complex to implement:

- Direct mapped cache – good best-case time, but flaky in worst case

- Two-way set associative cache

- Two-way skewed associative cache

- Four-way set associative cache

- Eight-way set associative cache, a common choice for later implementations

- 12-way set associative cache, similar to eight-way

- Fully associative cache – the best miss rates, but practical only for a small number of entries

6.4.4.1 Direct Mapped Cache

With this cache organization, each location in main memory can go in only one entry in the cache. Therefore, a direct-mapped cache can also be called a "one-way set associative" cache. It does not have a replacement policy as such, since there is no choice of which cache entry's contents to evict. This means that if two locations map to the same entry, they may continually knock each other out. Although simpler, a direct-mapped cache needs to be much larger than an associative one to give comparable performance, and it is more unpredictable. Let x be block number in cache, y be block number of memory, and n be number of blocks in cache, then mapping is done with the help of the equation $x = y \bmod n$.

6.4.4.2 Two-Way Set Associative Cache

If each location in main memory can be cached in either of two locations in the cache, one logical question is: *which one of the two?* The simplest and most commonly used scheme, shown in the right-hand diagram above, is to use the least significant bits of the memory location's index as the index for the cache memory, and to have two entries for each index. One benefit of this scheme is that the tags stored in the cache do not have to include that part of the main memory address which is implied by the cache memory's index. Since the cache tags have fewer bits, they require fewer transistors, take less space on the processor circuit board or on the microprocessor chip, and can be read and compared faster. Also, LRU is especially simple since only one bit needs to be stored for each pair.

6.4.4.3 Speculative Execution[23]

One of the advantages of a direct mapped cache is that it allows simple and fast speculation. Once the address has been computed, the one cache index which might have a copy of that location in memory is known. That cache entry can be read, and the processor can continue to work with that data before it finishes checking that the tag actually matches the requested address.

The idea of having the processor use the cached data before the tag match completes can be applied to associative caches as well. A subset of the tag, called a *hint*, can be used to pick just one of the possible cache entries mapping to the requested address. The entry selected by the hint can then be used in parallel with checking the full tag. The hint technique works best when used in the context of address translation, as is explained in the footnote below.

---

[23] **Speculative execution** is an optimization technique where a computer system performs some task that may not be needed. Work is done before it is known whether it is actually needed, so as to prevent a delay that would have to be incurred by doing the work after it is known that it is needed. If it turns out the work was not needed after all, most changes made by the work are reverted and the results are ignored

6.4.5 Cache Miss

A cache miss is a failed attempt to read or write a piece of data in the cache,. A cache miss results in a main memory access with much longer latency. There are three kinds of cache misses: instruction read miss, data read miss, and data write miss.

Cache read misses from an *instruction* cache generally cause the largest delay, because the processor, or at least the thread of execution, must wait (stall) until the instruction is fetched from main memory.

Cache read misses from a *data* cache usually cause a smaller delay, because instructions not dependent on the cache read can be issued and continue execution until the data is returned from main memory, and the dependent instructions can resume execution.

Cache write misses to a *data* cache generally cause the shortest delay, because the write can be queued and there are few limitations on the execution of subsequent instructions; the processor can continue until the queue is full.

6.5 Disk Cache

A *disk cache* is a mechanism for improving the time it takes to read from or write to a hard disk. Today, a disk cache is usually included as part of the hard disk, in which case it can also be called a *disk buffer*. A disk cache can also be a specified portion of random access memory (RAM). In this case it can also be referred to as a *soft* disk cache or a *page cache*. The disk cache holds data that has recently been read and, in some cases, adjacent data areas that are likely to be accessed next.

A disk cache enables faster processing of reading/writing, commands and other input and output process between the hard disk, the memory and computing components.

A disk buffer, as an integrated part of the hard disk, is now a standard feature of most hard disk drives. The size of disk buffer ranges from 128 MB in standard disks to 1 GB in solid state disks.

Typically, a disk cache stores the most recent and frequently used programs and data. When a user or program requests data, the operating system first reviews the disk cache. If the data is found, the OS and memory quickly deliver the data to the program.

Pages in the page cache modified after being brought in are called dirty pages. Since non-dirty pages in the page cache have identical copies in secondary storage (e.g. hard disk drive or solid-state drive), discarding and reusing their space is much quicker than paging out application memory, and is often preferred over flushing the dirty pages into secondary storage and reusing their space. Executable binaries, such as applications and libraries, are also typically accessed through page cache and mapped to individual process spaces using virtual memory (on Unix like systems this is done through the mmap system). This means that the binary files are shared between separate processes, but also that unused parts of binaries will be flushed out of main memory eventually, leading to memory conservation.

Since cached pages can be easily evicted and re-used, some operating systems (notably Windows NT) even report the page cache usage as "available" memory, while the memory is actually allocated to disk pages. This has led to some confusion about the utilization of page cache in Windows.

Dirty pages (pages whose content has been changed, so that it no longer matches the content of the associated section on disk) in cache have to be flushed to disk before they can be freed. When a file write occurs, the cached page for the particular block is looked up. If it is already found in the page cache, the write is done to that page in the main memory. If it is not found in the page cache, then, if the write perfectly falls on page boundaries, the page is does not even have to be read from disk. Space can be allocated and immediately marked dirty. Otherwise, the page(s) are fetched from disk and requested modifications are done.

6.6 Dynamic Linking

A **dynamic linker** is the part of an operating system that loads and links the shared libraries needed by executables when they are executed (at "run time"), by copying the necessary content of libraries from persistent storage to RAM, relocating pointers and making any other address references needed in the using executable. The specific operating system and executable format determine how the dynamic linker functions and how it is implemented.

A dynamic linker is a special part of an operating system that loads external shared libraries into a running process and then binds those shared libraries dynamically to the running process. This approach is also called **dynamic linking** or **late linking**. Since the dynamic linker has identified the locations and address of the library content, it can use the same instance for multiple executables[24], thus economizing memory use.

6.7 Exercises

6.7.1 Virtual memory systems depend on the principle of locality for their utility. In what kind of a system might the principle *not* hold? How would that affect the operation of a virtual memory system?

6.7.2 Section 6.1 describes the physical configuration of a hard disk. More and more secondary storage is using SSD technology. How might this kind of technology affect the effectiveness of paging and the implementation of paging for such a system?

6.7.3 Describe a memory reference on a system with cache memory, virtual memory and disk cache.

6.7.4 Would a segmented memory addressing system be more appropriate than a paging system for a system using an SSD for secondary storage?

6.7.5 With **NRU** (Not Recently Used) page replacement algorithm, the "not referenced but modified" status is chosen over the "referenced but not modified" status. Would not reversing these priorities result in less copying of modified segments back to secondary storage, and thus faster execution? Discuss why the existing priority scheme might have been chosen.

6.7.6 The text states that "Replacement Policies for cache are, *for the most part*, very similar to those for virtual memory" In what ways might they be different?

---

[24] Assuming the library unit is designed to support concurrent utilization.

6.8 Questions

6.8.1 True-False

6.8.1.1 RAM is much cheaper than external storage

6.8.1.2 Virtual memory adds to the complexity of the operating systems

6.8.1.3 The CPU can only deal directly with locations in primary storage.

6.8.1.4 When a process begins execution in a virtual memory system implemented by paging, all of the pages containing sections of the process must be called into memory in order to establish a system of virtual addresses to be used in executing the process.

6.8.1.5 Locality of reference has strengthened for user software. This is mostly attributed to the spread of object-oriented programming techniques that emphasize unified structures.

6.8.1.6 Page replacement in modern kernels (Linux, FreeBSD, and Solaris) tends to work at the level of a general purpose kernel memory allocator, rather than at the higher level of a virtual memory subsystem.

6.8.1.7 Pages usually correspond to natural divisions of a program such as individual routines or data tables, so paging is generally more visible to the programmer than segmentation

6.8.1.8 Segmentation is incompatible with virtual memory

6.8.1.9 Virtual memory systems using segmentation will be much less subject to thrashing than will paging systems

6.8.1.10 Replacement policies for cache are, for the most part, quite different from those for virtual memory

6.8.2 Multiple Choice

6.8.2.1 Virtual memory systems are subject to _____, which occurs when the computer's virtual memory resources become saturated, leading to a constant state of exchanging data in memory for data on disk,
   a. whiplash
   b. thrashing
   c. rocking
   d. bouncing
   e. none of the above

6.8.2.2 There are a number of possible strategies for choosing a page to swap out. One of them, _____ is relatively easy to implement. Unfortunately, in many systems this algorithm has been seen to target popular library functions used by many processes
a.   CLOCK
b.   LFU
c.   NRU
d.   FIFO
e.   none of the above

6.8.2.3 The replacement policy decides where in the cache a copy of a particular entry of main memory will go. If the replacement policy is free to choose any entry in the cache to hold the copy, the cache is called _____ *associative.*
a.   *completely*
b.   *totally*
c.   *fully*
d.   *entirely*
e.   none of the above

6.8.3   Completion

6.8.3.1 Systems can use disk space as an extension of their memory space (_____ memory systems)

6.8.3.2   The principle of locality states that memory references by the processor tend to

_____

6.8.3.3   The time it takes for the desired sector to rotate to a position under the read/write head is called rotational _____

6.8.3.4 In a paging system, a program references a word by means of a(n) _____ *address,* which is implemented as a *page number* and an *offset* within the page

6.8.3.5 There are a number of possible strategies for choosing a page to swap out. With one of them, _____ page references closer to the current time have more impact than earlier page references. This ensures that pages referenced more recently, even though less frequently, will have higher priority over pages frequently referenced in the past

6.8.3.6 Memory _____ is the division of a computer's primary memory sections. Unlike pages which are not generally of uniform sizes, and are generally controlled by programmers, rather than the operating system

6.8.3.7 It is not cost effective to build computers in which all of the RAM is of high speed technology, but it is possible to include a relatively small section using high speed RAM (such a section is called a _____.)

6.8.3.8   _____ **execution** is an optimization technique where a computer system performs some task that may not be needed

7. Organization of Information

Computers are digital devices and information is represented in binary format, using 0's or 1's (bits.)

Since the amount of information that can be represented using a single bit is so limited, computing systems typically use *combinations* of bits.

Some of these combinations are known as bytes, words, doublewords, blocks, pages and files. Each is used to represent and or manipulate some kinds of information (in some cases *several* different kinds of information in the same combinatorial unit.)

7.1 Bytes

The **byte,** as a unit of digital information, now usually assumed to consist of eight bits.

Historically, the term *byte* was initially used to mean the number of bits used to encode a single character of text in a computer. In many computer architectures, however, the term was used to refer to the smallest addressable unit of memory.

Historically, then, the size of a byte has been hardware dependent and no definitive standards existed mandating the size.

(byte-sizes from 1 to 48 bits are known to have been used.)

Many early character encoding systems used six bits, and machines using six-bit and nine-bit bytes were common into the 1960s. These machines most commonly had memory words of 12, 24, 36, 48 or 60 bits, corresponding to two, four, six, eight or 10 of the six-bit bytes.

The modern *de-facto* standard of eight bits (as documented in ISO/IEC 2382-1:1993) is a convenient power of two and supports the representation, as decimal integers, the values 0 through 255 for one byte. Many types of applications use information representable in eight or fewer bits and processor designers optimize for this common usage. The popularity of major commercial computing architectures has aided in the ubiquitous acceptance of the eight-bit size.

The development of eight-bit microprocessors in the 1970s also helped popularize this storage size.

Microprocessors such as the Intel 8008 (the direct predecessor of the 8080 and the 8086) used in early personal computers, could also perform a small number of operations on the four-bit pairs in a byte

(operations such as the decimal-add-adjust DAA instruction.)

A four-bit quantity is often called a nibble (also *nybble*) which is conveniently represented by a single hexadecimal digit.

Many programming languages define the data type *byte*.

In data transmission systems, the byte is defined as a contiguous sequence of bits in a serial data stream representing the smallest distinguished unit of data. A transmission unit might include start bits, stop bits, or parity bits, and thus could vary from 7 to 12 bits to contain a single 7-bit ASCII code.

In most common architectures, each byte in memory has an address, identifying its location, and each combination of bytes (each word, etc.) will also have an address derived from the addresses of the bytes from which it is constituted.

7.2 Words (and Doublewords)

In computing, the term **word** refers to the natural unit of data used by a particular processor design. It does not have an accepted standard size, but refers to a fixed-sized piece of data handled as a unit by the instruction set or the hardware of a processor. The number of bits in a word (the *word size*, *word width*, or *word length*) is an important characteristic of any specific processor design or computer architecture.

Modern architectures typically use 32 bit or 64-bit words, built of four or eight bytes.

The size of a word is reflected in many aspects of a computer's structure and operation; the majority of the registers in a processor are usually word sized and the largest piece of data that can be transferred to and from the working memory in a single operation is a word in many architectures (not all architectures. The Intel 8088 was one noteworthy exception.) The largest possible address size, used to designate a location in memory, is typically a hardware word (here, "hardware word" means the full-sized natural word of the processor, as opposed to any other definition used).

Modern processors (including embedded systems) usually have a word size of 8, 16, 24, 32, or 64 bits, while modern general purpose computers usually use 32 or 64 bits. Special purpose digital processors may use other sizes, and many other sizes have been used historically, including 9, 12, 18, 24, 26, 36, 39, 40, 48, and 60 bits. Several of the earliest computers (and a few modern as well) use binary-coded decimal (BCD) rather than plain binary. These typically have a word size of 10 or 12 decimal digits. Some early decimal computers had no fixed word length at all.

The size of a word can sometimes differ from the expected in order to support backward compatibility with earlier computers. If multiple compatible variations or a family of processors share a common architecture and instruction set but have different word sizes, their documentation and software may become notationally complex to accommodate the difference.

7.3 Cache Blocks/Cache Lines

A *cache* is a section of smaller, faster memory, which stores copies of the data from frequently used main memory locations. Most CPUs have different independent caches, including instruction and data caches. The data cache is usually organized as a hierarchy of more cache levels (L1, L2, etc.).

Data is transferred between memory and cache in blocks of fixed size, called *cache lines* or *cache blocks*. When a cache line is copied from memory into the cache, a cache entry is created. The cache entry will include the copied data as well as an identification (called a tag) of the location in main memory of which that block/line is a copy.

When the processor needs to read or write a location in main memory, it first checks for a corresponding entry in the cache. The cache checks for the contents of the requested memory location in any cache lines that might contain that address. If the processor finds that the memory location is in the cache, a *cache hit* has occurred. However, if the processor does not find the memory location in the cache, a *cache miss* has occurred. In the case of a cache hit, the processor immediately makes use of the data in the cache line. For a cache miss, the cache allocates a new entry and copies data from main memory, then the request is fulfilled, using the contents of the cache.

Example

The original Pentium 4 had a 4-way set associative L1 data cache of size 8 KB with 64 byte cache blocks. Hence, there are 8KB/64 = 128 cache blocks, and, being 4-way set associative, this implies 128/4=32 sets (and hence $2^5 = 32$ different indices). There are $64=2^6$ possible offsets.

Since the CPU address is 32 bits, this implies 32=21+5+6, and hence 21 bits of tag field.

The original Pentium 4 also had an 8-way set associative L2 integrated cache of size 256 KB with 128 byte cache blocks.

This implies 32=17+8+7, and hence 17 bits of tag field.

As indicated above, different systems will have cache blocks of different sizes (and, in fact different caches on the same system will use blocks of different sizes.)

7.4 Pages

With the development of virtual memory systems (and disk cache systems) it became desirable to divide system RAM into sections of uniform sizes related to amount of information that could be conveniently (and relatively efficiently) read from and/or written to a hard disk.

These subdivisions came to be referred to as "*pages*"

7.4.1 Tracks, Sectors and Clusters[xxiii]

In computer disk storage, a **sector** is a subdivision of a **track** on a magnetic disk or optical disc. Each sector stores a fixed amount of user-accessible data, (traditionally 512 bytes for hard disk drives and 2048 bytes for CD-ROMs and DVD-ROMs. Newer HDDs use 4096-byte sectors, which are known as the Advanced Format, *AF*).

The sector is the minimum physical storage unit of a hard drive. Most disk partitioning schemes are designed to have files occupy an integral number of sectors regardless of the file's actual size. Files that do not fill out an integral number of sectors will have the remainder of their last sector filled with zeroes.

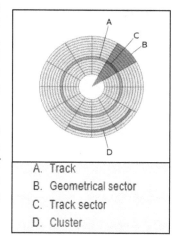

A. Track
B. Geometrical sector
C. Track sector
D. Cluster

To reduce the overhead of managing on-disk data structures, the filesystem does not allocate individual disk sectors by default, but contiguous groups of sectors, called *clusters*. On a disk that uses 512-byte sectors, a 512-byte cluster contains one sector, whereas a 4-KB cluster contains eight sectors. A cluster is the smallest logical amount of disk space that will be allocated to hold a file. (The term *cluster* was changed to *allocation unit* in DOS 4.0 but the term *cluster* is still widely used.

7.4.2 Page Sizes[xxiv]

The process of reading from or writing to a (magnetic) disk involves two steps, first moving the read/write head to the correct track, and then waiting until the desired sector rotates into position for the head to read from it or write to it. Moving the head to the correct track generally takes more time (latency) than it does for the sector to arrive to the read/write head (rotational delay) and so it is efficient (takes less data transfer time) to store data that tends to be referenced together on the same track.

Computer	Page Size
Atlas	512 48-bit words
Honeywell-Multics	1024 36-bit words
IBM 370/XA and 370/ESA	4 Kbytes
VAX family	512 bytes
IBM AS/400	512 bytes
DEC Alpha	8 Kbytes
MIPS	4 Kbytes to 16 Mbytes
UltraSPARC	8 Kbytes to 4 Mbytes
Pentium	4 Kbytes or 4 Mbytes
IBM POWER	4 Kbytes
Itanium	4 Kbytes to 256 Mbytes

Some Page Sizes

It is the basic idea of virtual memory systems to store and load sections of data that will be referenced together. It makes sense to store and load data together as pages onto and from the same track, and so it is reasonable that pages be multiples of the sector size that the hard disks of the system use.

7.5 Segments

Memory segmentation is the division of a computer's primary memory into **segments** or **sections**.

Memory segmentation is similar to paging, but pages are of uniform size and segments can be of different sizes.

In a computer system using segmentation, a reference to a memory location includes a value that identifies a segment and an offset (memory location) within that segment.

Segments usually correspond to natural divisions of a program such as individual routines or data tables, so segmentation is generally more visible to the programmer than is paging. Different segments may be created for different program modules, or for different classes of memory usage such as code and data segments. Segments are also often designed to be shared between different programs.

7.6 Files, Directories, Subdirectories, File Manager

A **computer file** is a computer resource for recording data in a computer storage device. In the same way that words can be written on paper, information can be written to a computer file.

There are different types of computer files, designed for different purposes. A file may be designed to store a picture, a written message, a video, a computer program, or any of a wide variety of other kinds of data. Some types of files can store several types of information at once (multimedia files for example.)

By using computer programs, a person can open, read, change, and close a computer file. An OS file manager will allow computer files to be reopened, modified, and copied any number of times.

Typically, files are organized in a file system, which keeps track of where the files are located on disk and enables user access.

On most modern operating systems, files are organized into one-dimensional arrays of bytes. The format of a file is defined by its content since a file is just a container for data. On some platforms the file format is dictated by its filename extension which will specify the rules for how the bytes in the file should be organized and interpreted. On most platforms, however, the extension does not "dictate" the organization but is, rather" more in the nature of a "hint" to the user as to the type of content in the file.

For example, the bytes of a plain text file (.txt in Windows) are associated with either ASCII or UTF-8 character encodings, while the bytes of image, video, and audio files are interpreted in other, very different ways.

Most file types also allocate a few bytes for metadata[25], which allows a file to carry some basic information about itself.

Information in a computer file can consist of smaller packets of information (often called "records" or "lines") that are individually different but share some common traits. For example, a payroll file might contain information concerning all the employees in a company and their payroll details; each record in the payroll file concerns just one employee, and all the records have the common trait of being related to payroll—this is very similar to placing all payroll information into a specific filing cabinet in an office that does not have a computer. A text file may contain lines of text, corresponding to printed lines on a piece of paper. Alternatively, a file may contain an arbitrary binary image (a BLOB) or it may contain an *executable*[26].

---

[25] Metadata is data [information] that provides information about other data

[26] In computing, **executable code** or an **executable file** or **executable program**, sometimes simply referred to as an **executable** or **binary**, causes a computer "to perform indicated tasks according to encoded instructions," as opposed to a data file that must be parsed by some program to be meaningful.

The most basic operations that programs can perform on a file are:
- Create a new file
- Change the access permissions and attributes of a file
- Open a file, which makes the file contents available to the program
- Read data from a file
- Write data to a file
- Close a file, terminating the association between it and the program

7.7 RAID Systems

When relatively inexpensive, albeit smaller[27] and, in many cases less reliable, hard disks started to be marketed, it was recognized that by using a collection of several smaller less expensive hard disks instead of just one large disk, one could create a *system* having a large capacity. Such a system could have several advantages:

Price: It was usually possible to buy large storage capacity as a combination of smaller cheaper drives for less money than a single high capacity drive would cost. The smaller drives were manufactured in large quantities, which resulted in economies of scale. The smaller drives were also more readily available.

Reliability: With several different drives, it is possible to put duplicate data on more than one drive. Then, if one drive were to fail, its data would not be lost.

Access Speed: With data in a large file stored on different drives, the system can access different portions of the file from the different drives simultaneously, resulting in faster access times than would be possible with one single drive.

In a RAID system (Redundant Array of Inexpensive Disks), data can be distributed across the drives in several different ways, referred to as RAID levels. These levels vary according to the required level of redundancy and performance.

The different schemes, or data distribution layouts, are named by the word RAID followed by a number, for example RAID 0 or RAID 1.

Each scheme, or RAID level, provides a different balance among the key goals: reliability, availability, performance, and capacity.

RAID levels greater than RAID 0 provide protection against unrecoverable sector read errors, as well as against failures of entire physical drives

---

[27] In the sense of having less storage capacity

7.7.1 RAID 0 Striping[xxv]

RAID 0 has no redundancy, and so does not provide improved reliability. It does, however, provide improved access speed.

A large file would be divided into several different *stripes*. Different stripes would be stored on different drives. When uploading or downloading the file multiple stripes could be uploaded/downloaded simultaneously, resulting in much improved I/O rates.

A RAID 0 array of n drives provides data read and write transfer rates up to n times as high as the individual drive rates, but it provides no data redundancy. As a result, RAID 0 is primarily used in applications, such as scientific computing or computer gaming, that require high performance but can tolerate lower reliability.

7.7.2 RAID 1 Mirroring[xxvi]

RAID 1 consists of having exact copies/mirrors of a set of data on two or more disks. In the illustration, there are two copies of one disk, but there can be more disks (i.e. for either disk, we could substitute another RAID system.)

RAID 1 does not use parity or striping across the mirrored disks. This layout is useful when read performance or reliability is more important than write performance or storage capacity.

The array will continue to operate so long as at least one member drive is operational.

Any read request can be serviced and handled by any drive in the array; thus, depending on the nature of I/O load, random read performance of a RAID 1 array may be as good as the sum of each member's performance (different portions of a file can be read from different disks, simultaneously, but the write performance remains at the level of a single disk, since a write operation must go to both disks (although simultaneously.)

RAID 1 systems require twice as many disks as do RAID 0 systems to achieve the same storage capacity.

7.7.3 RAID 2 Bit Level Striping with Parity[xxvii]

RAID 2, which is rarely used in practice, stripes data at the bit (rather than block) level, and uses a Hamming code for error correction. The disks are synchronized by the controller to spin at the same angular orientation and it

generally cannot service multiple requests simultaneously. Extremely high data transfer rates are possible.

With all hard disk drives implementing internal error correction, the complexity of an external Hamming code offered little advantage over parity so RAID 2 has been rarely implemented; it is the only original level of RAID that is not currently used.

7.7.4 RAID 3 Byte Level Striping with Parity Disk[xxviii]

RAID 3 is also rarely used in practice. It consists of byte-level striping with a dedicated parity disk. One of the characteristics of RAID 3 is that it generally cannot service multiple requests simultaneously. This is because any single block of data will, be spread across all members of the set and will be positioned in the same location. Therefore, virtually any I/O operation

requires activity on every disk (and usually requires synchronized spindles, as well.)

This makes RAID 3 suitable for applications that demand the highest transfer rates in long sequential reads and writes (video editing, for example.) Applications that make small reads and writes from random disk locations will get the worst performance out of this level.

This level provides no significant advantages over other RAID levels, so it is, in fact, now obsolete. Both RAID 3 and RAID 4 were quickly replaced by RAID 5.

7.7.5 RAID 4 Block Level Striping with Parity Disk[xxix]

RAID 4 consists of block-level striping with a dedicated parity disk. RAID 4 provides good performance of reads, but the performance doing writes is low because of the need to write all parity data to a single disk.

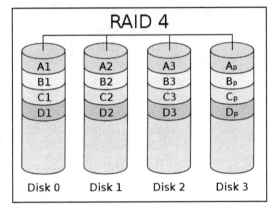

In the diagram, a read request for block A1 would be serviced by disk 0. A simultaneous read request for block B1 would have to wait, but a read request for B2 could be serviced concurrently by disk 1.

7.7.6 RAID 5 block-level striping with distributed parity[xxx]

RAID 5 consists of block-level striping with distributed parity. Unlike in RAID 4, parity information is distributed among the drives. It requires that all drives but one be present to operate. Upon failure of a single drive, subsequent reads can be calculated from the distributed parity and no data would be lost. RAID 5 requires at least three disks.

In comparison to RAID 4, RAID 5's distributed parity evens out the stress of a dedicated parity disk among all RAID members. Additionally, write performance is increased since all RAID members participate in the serving of write requests. Although it won't be as efficient as a striping (RAID 0) setup, because, although parity must still be written, this is no longer the bottleneck it is in RAID 4.

Since parity calculation is performed on the full stripe, small changes to the array experience *write amplification*: in the worst case when a single, logical sector is to be written, the original sector and the associated parity sector need to be read, the original data is removed from the parity, the new data calculated into the parity and both the new data sector and the new parity sector are written.

7.7.7 RAID 6 block-level striping with two parity blocks[xxxi]

RAID 6 extends RAID 5 by adding another parity block; so, it uses block-level striping with two parity blocks distributed across all member disks.

According to the Storage Networking Industry Association (SNIA), the definition of RAID 6 is: "Any form of RAID that can continue to execute read and

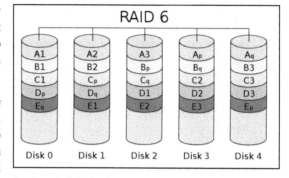

write requests to all of a RAID array's virtual disks in the presence of any two concurrent disk failures. Several methods, including dual check data computations (parity and Reed-Solomon[28]), orthogonal dual parity check data and diagonal parity, have been used to implement RAID Level 6."

RAID 6 does not have a performance penalty for read operations, but it does have a performance penalty on write operations because of the overhead associated with parity calculations. Performance varies greatly depending on how RAID 6 is implemented in the manufacturer's storage architecture—in software, firmware, or by using firmware and specialized ASICs for intensive parity calculations. RAID 6 can read up to the same speed as RAID 5 with the same number of physical drives.

---

[28] **Reed–Solomon codes** are a group of error-correcting codes that were introduced by Irving S. Reed and Gustave Solomon in 1960. They have many applications, the most prominent of which include consumer technologies such as CDs, DVDs, Blu-ray Discs, QR Codes, data transmission technologies such as DSL and WiMAX, broadcast systems such as DVB and ATSC, and storage systems such as RAID 6. They are also used in satellite communication.

7.8 Exercises

7.8.1 The text states "The largest possible address size, used to designate a location in memory, is typically a hardware word (here, "hardware word" means the full-sized natural word of the processor, as opposed to any other definition used)" What "other " definitions might have been considered for use?

7.8.2 Explain why computers using BCD typically use a word size of 10 or 12 decimal digits.

7.8.3 What would be the relative advantages and disadvantages of larger versus smaller cluster sizes?

7.8.4 Most file systems use file identifiers with file extensions that indicate the type of data in the file. In some systems these extensions are "hints" or "suggestions" and in some systems the file format is dictated by its filename extension. What are the advantages and disadvantages of each type of system?

7.9 Questions

7.9.1 True-False

7.9.1.1 The size of the byte has historically been hardware dependent and no definitive standards existed that mandated the size.

7.9.1.2 Most disk partitioning schemes are designed to optimize disk storage capacity. Each file occupies only the portions of sectors required by data in the file.

7.9.1.3 RAID 0 systems require twice as many disks as do RAID 1 systems to achieve the same storage capacity.

7.9.2 Multiple Choice

7.9.2.1 A *word* is a fixed-sized piece of data handled as a unit by the instruction set or the hardware of the processor. The number of bits in a word (the word _____) is an important characteristic of any specific processor design or computer architecture
    a.   size
    b.   width
    c.   length
    d.   any of the above
    e.   none of the above

7.9.2.2 RAID _____ has no redundancy, and so does not provide improved reliability. It does, however, provide improved access speed.
    a.   0
    b.   1
    c.   4
    d.   5
    e.   none of the above

7.9.2.3   RAID _____ provides good performance of reads, but the performance doing writes is low because of the need to write all parity data to a single disk
   a.   0
   b.   1
   c.   4
   d.   5
   e.   none of the above

7.9.2.4   RAID _____ uses block-level striping with two parity blocks distributed across all member disks
   a.   0
   b.   1
   c.   4
   d.   5
   e.   none of the above

7.9.3   Completion

7.9.3.1   Computers are _____ devices and information is represented in binary format

7.9.3.2   The _____ as a unit of digital information most commonly consists of eight bits. Historically, it was the number of bits used to encode a single character of text in a computer and in many computer architectures, the term has often been used to mean the smallest addressable unit of memory

7.9.3.3   In computing, a(n) _____ is the natural unit of data used by a particular processor design.

7.9.3.4   A data cache is usually organized as a(n) _____ of cache levels: (L1, L2, etc.).

7.9.3.5   When the processor needs to read or write a location in main memory, it first checks for a corresponding entry in the cache. The cache checks for the contents of the requested memory location in any cache lines that might contain that address. If the processor finds that the memory location is in the cache, a cache _____ has occurred. In this case, the processor immediately reads or writes the data in the cache line.

7.9.3.6   In computer disk storage, a(n) _____ is a subdivision of a **track** on a magnetic disk or optical disk.

7.9.3.7   On some platforms the file format is dictated by its filename _____.

7.9.3.8   _____ is data [information] that provides information about other data.

8. Security and Antivirus, Encryption and Decryption

Our daily lives, economic safety, and even national security have come to depend on stable, safe, and resilient computer and communication systems. Thus, computer security is an extremely important issue.

By *computer security*, we basically mean the maintenance of system integrity and the availability and confidentiality of information dealt with by the computer system. The operating system plays a paramount role in the overall security of any system.

8.1 Security Issues

The main security issues that an operating system might be expected to deal with are issues of:

Authenticity

Availability

Confidentiality

Data integrity.

8.2 Sources of Threats to System Security

One of the functions of an operating system is to provide a level of security, and so, the system should work to defend against:

physical malfunctions

user errors

attacks from external sources.

The security within a computer system can be divided into various layers such as maintaining:

the security of the information the system holds

the physical security of the system,

the security of the network in which it operates.

8.2.1 Physical Malfunctions

The operating system cannot, of course, *prevent* physical malfunctions, so its role in this regard would be limited to *detecting* the malfunctions when they occur[29], and limiting their damage to the information in the system.

Data *storage* is subject to errors, and so is data *transmission*.

---

[29]   And they WILL occur.

8.2.1.1 Data errors

In a digital system, a data error will take the form of either a 0 stored (or transmitted) when the correct value would have been 1 or a 1 stored/transmitted instead of a 0. Such errors can be due to manufacturing defects, wear, environmental EMF, and many other factors.

8.2.1.1.1 Error Detection and Correction

Most operating systems utilize forms of error detection, and many also implement forms of error *correction*.

These techniques enable reliable delivery and storage of digital data. Error *detection* techniques support *detection* of errors, while error *correction* enables *reconstruction* of the original data (at least in many cases.)

8.2.1.1.1.1 Redundancy

Error detection/correction is generally achieved by adding some redundancy (i.e., some extra data) to the data. Users can utilize the extra to check consistency of the data, and, possibly, to recover data that might have been corrupted.

In such a scheme, a number of *check bits* (or *parity data*)
(derived from the data bits by some algorithm)
are added to the data. A user can simply apply the same algorithm to the data bits and compare the result with the check bits. If the values do not match, an error must have occurred.

Many such algorithms also support error correction, i.e. they can be used to identify which data bits had erroneous values. (Since the only values are 0 and 1, the correct value is trivially identified. If the data value is 0 and it is wrong, the correct value must have been 1. If the data value is 1 and it is erroneous, then the correct value must be 0.)

8.2.1.1.1.2 Parity bits

A *parity bit* is a bit that is added to a group of source/data bits to ensure that the number of *set* bits
(i.e., bits with value 1)
in the outcome is even or odd.

This is a very simple scheme for detecting single
(or any other odd number i.e., three, five, etc.)
of errors in the group of data bits.

If, however, there were an *even* number of flipped bits, the parity bit would fail to indicate any error, even though the data *would*, in fact, contain errors.

8.2.1.1.1.3 Checksums

A *checksum* of a collection (of a fixed word length) of data is a modular arithmetic sum of that data. Such a sum may be negated by means of a ones'-complement operation, which provides a very efficient operation which will result in all zero data unless there is an error.

Checksum schemes include parity bits, check digits, and longitudinal redundancy checks.

Some checksum schemes are specifically designed to detect errors commonly introduced by humans when writing down or remembering identification numbers.

8.2.1.1.1.4 Data Storage

Error detection and correction codes are often used to improve the reliability of data storage media.
(In fact, a "parity track" was present on the first magnetic tape data storage in 1951.)

The "Optimal Rectangular Code" used in group coded recording tapes not only detects but also corrects single-bit errors. Some file formats, (particularly archive formats), include a checksum system (most often CRC32) to detect corruption and truncation and can employ redundancy and/or parity files to recover portions of corrupted data.

Reed Solomon codes[30] are used in compact discs to correct errors caused by scratches.

Modern hard drives use CRC codes to detect minor errors in sector reads, and Reed–Solomon codes to correct them. They are also used to recover data from sectors that have "gone bad" and store that data in spare sectors.

---

[30] **Reed–Solomon codes** are a group of error-correcting codes that were introduced by Irving S. Reed and Gustave Solomon in 1960. They have many applications, the most prominent of which include consumer technologies such as CDs, DVDs, Blu-ray Discs, QR Codes, data transmission technologies such as DSL and WiMAX, broadcast systems such as DVB and ATSC, and storage systems such as RAID 6. They are also used in satellite communication.

RAID systems use a variety of error correction techniques to correct errors when a hard drive completely fails. Some filesystems, as well as some RAID implementations, support data scrubbing[31] and resilvering[32], which allows bad blocks to be detected and (hopefully) recovered before they are used. The recovered data may be re-written to exactly the same physical location, to spare blocks elsewhere on the same piece of hardware, or the data may be rewritten onto replacement hardware.

8.2.1.1.1.5 Error-correcting memory

DRAM memory may provide increased protection by relying on built in error correcting codes. This kind of error-correcting memory (known as *ECC* or *EDAC-protected* memory) is particularly desirable for applications, such as servers, which cannot tolerate errors, as well as deep-space applications which suffer relatively high rates of RAM errors due to high radiation levels.

Error-correcting memory controllers traditionally use *Hamming codes*, although some use *triple modular redundancy*.

8.2.1.1.1.6 *Interleaving*

Interleaving can ameliorate the effect of a single radiation event, keeping it from modifying multiple bits in physically neighboring words. It associates neighboring bits to different words.

As long as a *single event upset* (SEU) does not exceed the error threshold (e.g., a single error) in any particular word between accesses, it can be corrected, by a single-bit error correcting code, and the illusion of an error-free memory system may be maintained.

8.2.1.1.1.7 Error Reporting

In addition to using hardware that provides features required for ECC memory to operate, operating systems usually have reporting facilities that are used to provide notifications when errors are transparently recovered. An increasing rate of such automatically corrected errors might indicate that a DIMM[33] module needs replacing, and such feedback information would not be easily available without the related reporting capabilities. One example is the Linux kernel's *EDAC* subsystem (previously known as *bluesmoke*), which collects the data from error-checking-enabled components inside a computer system; beside collecting and reporting back the events related to ECC memory, it also supports other checksumming errors, including those detected on the PCI bus.

A few systems also support *memory scrubbing*.

---

[31] data scrubbing is an error correction technique that uses a background task to periodically inspect main memory or storage for errors, then correct detected errors. Data scrubbing reduces the likelihood that single correctable errors will accumulate, leading to reduced risks of uncorrectable errors.

[32] Resilvering (also known as resyncing, rebuilding, or reconstructing) is the process of repairing a damaged device using the contents of healthy devices.

[33] **DIMM** or **dual in-line memory module** comprises a series of dynamic random-access memory integrated circuits. These modules are mounted on a printed circuit board and designed for use in personal computers, workstations and servers

8.2.1.1.1.8 Memory scrubbing

Memory scrubbing (similar to data scrubbing) consists of reading from each computer memory location, correcting bit errors (if any) with an error-correcting code (ECC) and, if necessary, writing the corrected data back to the same location.

Because of the high integration density of modern computer memory chips, the individual memory cell structures became small enough to be vulnerable to cosmic rays and/or alpha particle emission. The errors caused by these phenomena are called *soft errors*. Over 8% of DIMM modules experience at least one such correctable error per year, and this can be a problem for DRAM and SRAM based memories. The probability of a soft error at any individual memory bit is very small. However, together with the large amount of memory modern computers (and especially servers) are equipped with, and together with extended periods of uptime, the probability of soft errors in the total memory installed is significant.

The information in an ECC memory is stored redundantly enough to correct single bit error per memory word, which is good enough to support the scrubbing of the memory content. If the memory controller scans systematically through the memory, the single bit errors can be detected, the erroneous bits can be identified using the ECC checksum, and the corrected data can be written back to the memory.

8.2.1.1.2 Error Recovery

One of the most important aspects of an operating system is an ability to continue to operate when errors have occurred or to resume operation after errors have occurred.

Many techniques are used to facilitate error recovery. These include:

Designing systems to be able to operate without some of its hardware components.

Implementing capabilities for error detection and correction.

Storing multiple copies of critical data in separate locations that are unlikely to suffer simultaneous damage.

When computer files contain information that is extremely important, a *back-up* process is used to protect against disasters that might destroy the files.

Backing up files simply involves making copies of the files and keeping copies in a separate location so that they can be restored if something happens to the computer, or if they are deleted accidentally.

There are many ways to back up files. Most computer systems provide utility programs to assist in the back-up process, which can become very time-consuming if there are many files to safeguard. Files are often copied to removable media such as writable CDs or cartridge tapes. Copying files to another hard disk in the same computer protects against failure of one disk, but if it is necessary to protect against failure or destruction of the entire computer, then copies of the files must be made on other media that can be removed from the computer and stored in a safe, distant location.

The grandfather-father-son backup method involves making three back-ups; the grandfather file is the oldest copy of the file and the son is the current copy.

8.3 User Errors

Humans do things they shouldn't. Sometimes they do them by mistake, sometimes they do them out of ignorance and sometimes they do them intentionally. We can never completely eliminate these human errors, but we can minimize them (or at least contain their effects) with a with a robust user authentication system and user access security system

to ensure that only authorized users have access to the system,

and that the authorized users only have access to resources for which they have approval.

8.3.1 Security incidents involving Human Error

All humans make mistakes:

One of the most intriguing findings from IBM's "2014 Cyber Security Intelligence Index" is that **95 percent of all security incidents involve human error**. Many of these are successful security attacks from external attackers who prey on human weakness in order to lure insiders within organizations to unwittingly provide them with access to sensitive information.

These mistakes are costly since they tend to involve the insiders with access to the most sensitive information. According to research by Federal Computer Week cited in a recent Vormetric report, the greatest impacts of successful security attacks involving insiders are exposure of sensitive data, theft of intellectual property and the introduction of malware. The research also reported that 59 percent of respondents agree that most information technology security threats that directly result from insiders are the result of innocent mistakes rather than malicious abuse of privileges.

8.3.2 Security Controls

One of the leading errors made by insiders is the sending of sensitive documents to unintended recipients. This is relatively easy to prevent by deploying security controls to monitor sensitive information being leaked out of the organization. Once these controls were considered complex to deploy, but in recent years, vendors have made them much easier to implement. This has dramatically reduced the level of user involvement required and increased their use.

These tools can also prevent users from engaging in inappropriate behavior, such as sending documents home via email or placing them on file-sharing sites or removable media such as USB sticks. Of course many people want to work from home (or other remote locations) and such tools make this difficult. The use of Virtual Private Networks (VPN's) allows the implementation of (at least some) of these tools to protect such remote work. These systems, of course, create their own security complications. (See 9.3.3)

Lost or stolen mobile devices are also a major concern and this is exacerbated by the growing trend toward the use of personal devices. Again, there is technology available to help organizations police what happens to data stored on devices. Some of this technology even allows sensitive data to be remotely wiped to prevent it from falling into the wrong hands.

8.3.3 Errors by Skilled Users

Human error is also a factor in other security incidents caused by insiders who are the most trusted and highly skilled (such as system and network administrators) and who are, therefore, capable of doing the most damage. According to IBM's report, some of the most commonly recorded forms of human error caused by such employees are system misconfigurations, poor patch management practices and the use of default names and passwords. There are a number of security controls that organizations should explore to guard against such threats.

8.3.4 Social Engineering

The human interest factor is also being exploited by attackers and plays a large part in successful security attacks seen today, but it is not always attributed to mistakes made by insiders. Many of these attacks involve social engineering techniques to lure individually targeted users into making mistakes. According to Verizon's "2013 Data Breach Investigations Report", 95 percent of advanced and targeted attacks involved spear-phishing scams with emails containing malicious attachments that can cause malware to be downloaded onto the user's computing device. This gives attackers a foothold into the organization from which they can search for valuable information, such as intellectual property.

8.3.5 Changing Tactics

There is evidence some that users might be mending their ways and falling prey less frequently to these kinds of attacks. Verizon's 2014 report found that the proportion of successful spearfishing security attacks has fallen to 78 percent.

Is this drop because users are becoming more savvy and are less likely to be lured into making such mistakes, or are attackers changing their tactics? It would appear that the latter is true since Verizon's 2014 report found a sizable increase in the use of strategic Web compromises as a method of gaining initial access. Malicious URL links contained in emails have long been a major vector of attacks, but users are becoming much more aware of such tactics — perhaps heeding advice not to trust such links.

8.3.6 Watering Hole Attacks

Today, legitimate websites are increasingly being hacked since they are just the sort of websites that users would routinely trust. However, compromised websites are also being used in attacks that target the interests of specific users or groups. There has also been a particular increase in so-called watering hole attacks — so named because they mimic the tactics of predators waiting at watering holes that their prey are likely to visit.

8.3.7 Technology Alone Is Not a Panacea

There are technologies available for organizations to help safeguard themselves against external factors that target individual users in hopes of causing them to make errors.

It is often said that any successful organization must focus on people, processes and technology in that order. Technology provides automated safeguards and processes to determine the series of actions to be taken to achieve a particular end but even organizations with strong security practices are vulnerable to human error. Often, not enough attention is paid to the "people" part of the equation. Technology and processes must be combined with employee education to stem errors made through social engineering and to raise awareness of the potential harm caused by carelessness. This makes employees aware of the threats they face and the part they are expected to play in guarding against them. Keeping organizations safe requires constantly educating employees about identifying suspicious communications and new possible risks.

8.3.8 User Access Security in Computing

"User access" refers to the mechanisms by which users gain access to system resources. In a computer system, the Operating System (OS) is the backbone of the computing environment and all resources are controlled and run from it. This means that the operating system is at the core of the entire system's security.

Security takes on many layers. Physical security to the computer system itself is one layer. Anyone within physical proximity to the computer can be a threat. Threats can also come from unauthorized access via the web, compromised applications, or poor user habits.

8.3.8.1 Securing User Access Using the Operating System

There are several different operating system security measures available to help maintain more secure user access. These include: placing limitations on user accounts, setting and enforcing secure password policies, establishing and controlling user permissions.

8.3.8.1.1 Limitations on User Accounts

This involves limiting the number of authorized users who have access to the operating system and related system applications.

Limiting access to the operating system enables better control of system administration, accountability and troubleshooting.

Limiting access to applications ensures access by the right users to the right applications only. The system must constantly be audited to keep access permissions up to date and especially to delete accounts of users who for one reason or another have left the company or business. Legacy accounts can be a huge security threat.

8.3.8.1.2 Password Policies

It is important to ensure that access to network servers, operating systems and applications is controlled using a system of passwords. This is one of many security layers, and one of the most basic forms of user access security to any system.

Enforcing good user password policies with emphasis on strong passwords combinations is key. With so many tools available online, simple passwords are easy to break and lead to system compromise.

Enforcing frequent password changes is also critical. Familiarity can always lead to compromise. If a user's password has been compromised, frequent changes will narrow the window of attack opportunity. A policy requiring frequent password changes will also identify legacy accounts and ensure that they do not become weak points in the system.

8.3.8.1.3 User Permissions

Many modern computer systems provide methods for protecting files against accidental and deliberate damage. Computers that have multiple users implement *file permissions* to control who may or may not modify, delete, or create files and folders. For example, a given user may be granted only permission to read a file or folder, but not to modify or delete it; or a user may be given permission to read and modify files or folders, but not to execute them. Permissions may also be used to allow only certain users to see the contents of a file or folder.

Permissions protect against unauthorized tampering or destruction of information in files and keep private information confidential from unauthorized users.

Another protection mechanism implemented in many computers is a *read-only flag*. When this flag is turned on for a file (which can be accomplished by a computer program or by a human user), the file can be examined, but it cannot be modified. This flag is useful for critical information that must not be modified or erased, such as special files that are used only by internal parts of the computer system. Some systems also include a *hidden* flag to make certain files invisible; this flag is used by the computer system to hide essential system files that users should not alter.

User permissions are defined simply as who has access to what. Although an application may have many authorized users, they do not all have the same level of access. In other words, some users or groups of users may have restricted access with the ability to only carry out a few functions. They may, for example, only be allowed to navigate within certain areas in an application. Other users may have more advanced privileges, enabling them to have full access to all operations within the system.

Ensuring that users have the minimum required permissions for them to perform their individual functions is the key. Unauthorized access and malicious attacks often need user access authentication. User permissions can determine the success of an attack and the damage extent. Accounts with administrative and super-user access are the most vulnerable.

Limiting access to approved users will not eliminate user errors, but it will tend to limit the effects of these errors, permitting any errors to affect only those resources for which that particular user has authorized access.

8.4 Measures to Protect System Security

Information security involves security of all data, all applications and of the operating system itself. All of these are sometimes in danger.

Threats may be due to mistakes by humans, malicious programs or persons, or, simply, existing system vulnerabilities. The following measures highlight the role of the operating system in maintaining security.

8.4.1 Authentication

Authentication is one of the protective methods used by OS to ensure that the user accessing a program is authorized or legitimate. An OS provides authentication using a number of techniques:

1. User names and passwords - these are names and passwords registered with the operating system to whom it allows access at the time of login.

2. Key Cards - these are physical cards programmed by the OS with unique identifying information that allows the user to login to the system.

3. User attributes - The operating system registers unique physical characteristics of the user (called attributes) to identify him at login. These may include fingerprints, signatures and eye retina patterns.

8.5 Attacks from External Sources

Cyberspace and its underlying infrastructure are vulnerable to a wide range of risk stemming from both physical and cyber threats and hazards. Sophisticated cyber actors (including even nation-states) regularly attempt to exploit vulnerabilities of digital systems to steal money and information, and are developing capabilities to disrupt, destroy, or threaten the delivery of essential services.

Information security threats come in many different forms. Some of the most common threats today are:

software attacks,

> Most computer users have experienced software attacks of some sort. Viruses, worms, phishing attacks, and Trojan horses are a few common examples of software attacks.

theft of intellectual property,

> The theft of intellectual property has also been an extensive issue for many businesses, especially those in the IT field.

identity theft,

> Identity theft is the attempt to act as someone else usually to obtain that person's personal information or to take advantage of their access to vital information.

theft of equipment or information,

> Theft of equipment or information is becoming more prevalent today because so many of our devices are mobile and can easily be stolen. They have also become far more desirable as their data storage capacity increases.

sabotage,

> Sabotage usually consists of the defacing (or even outright destruction) of an organization's website, often in an attempt to cause loss of customer confidence.

and information extortion.

> Information extortion consists of the theft of a company's property or information as an attempt to receive a payment in exchange for returning the information or property back to its owner, as with ransomware.

There are many ways to help protect against most of these attacks and one of the best is user carefulness. Nevertheless, a well designed OS will provide an extra level of protection against these external threats, as well as against human errors, programming errors and physical malfunctions.

The nature of the threats that concerns a system will vary greatly depending on the circumstances and on who or what organization runs the system, but the primary problem involves controlling *access* to computer systems and the information stored in them

8.6 Exercises

8.6.1 Passwords can become known to unauthorized users by a number of ways. Can you suggest a strategy for detecting use of passwords by unauthorized users?

8.6.2 Physical malfunctions will occur, and an operating system should detect their occurrences and take appropriate actions to limit damage. Suggest some classifications for physical malfunctions, explain how an operating system might detect when a malfunction of each given type has occurred and describe what might be an appropriate action to take in the event of a malfunction of that type.

8.6.3 The use of error detecting codes will slow the transmission/processing of data but allow a system to detect errors. It allows the system to take appropriate action in case of erroneous data but does not prevent the loss of the original information. The use of error correcting codes allows the system to identity errors and to reconstruct the original information but does so at cost of slower transmission/processing. Suggest some systems/situations in which the use of no error detecting, error detecting and error correcting would be appropriate. Explain why.

8.6.4 Checksum schemes include parity bits, check digits, and longitudinal redundancy checks. Describe the distinctions between these various schemes.

8.7 Questions

8.7.1 True-False

8.7.1.1 By computer security, we basically mean the maintenance of system integrity and the availability and confidentiality of information dealt with by the computer system. The operating system plays a paramount role in the overall security of the system.

8.7.1.2 A parity single bit can detect whether an even number of errors have occurred in a data set, but it will not detect an odd number of errors.

8.7.1.3 Systems have recently begun using error detection and correction codes to improve the reliability of data storage media.

8.7.1.4 Error detection and correction codes are often used to improve the reliability of data storage media. This is not a recent development. In fact, a "parity track" was present on the first magnetic tape data storage in 1951.)

8.7.1.5 Operating systems usually have reporting facilities that are used to provide notifications when errors are transparently recovered.

8.7.1.6 95 percent of all security incidents involve human error

8.7.1.7 Frequent password changes ensure that legacy accounts do not become weak points in the system

8.7.2 Multiple Choice

8.7.2.1 One of the functions of an operating system is to provide a level of security, and so, the system should work to defend against _____
a. physical malfunctions
b. user errors
c. attacks from external sources
d. all of the above
e. none of the above

8.7.2.2 Because of the high integration density of modern computer memory chips, the individual memory cell structures became small enough to be vulnerable to cosmic rays and/or alpha particle emission. The errors caused by these phenomena are called _____ errors.
   a. radiation
   b. EMF
   c. soft
   d. hard
   e. none of the above

8.7.2.3 According to a 2013 report 95 percent of advanced and targeted attacks involved spear-phishing scams with emails containing malicious attachments that can cause malware to be downloaded onto the user's computing device. report in 2014 showed that this proportion had fallen to ____ percent.
   a. 91
   b. 78
   c. 44
   d. 22
   e. none of the above

8.7.3 Completion

8.7.3.1 Data errors in a digital system can be due to manufacturing defects, wear, environmental _____, and many other factors

8.7.3.2 A(n) _____ bit is a bit that is added to a group of source/data bits to ensure that the number of *set* bits (i.e., bits with value 1) in the outcome is even or odd.

8.7.3.3 A(n) _____ of a collection (of a fixed word length) of data is a modular arithmetic sum of that data

8.7.3.4 Some file formats, (particularly archive formats), include a checksum (most often _____) to detect corruption and truncation

8.7.3.5 (also known as resyncing, rebuilding, or reconstructing) is the process of repairing a damaged device using the contents of healthy devices

8.7.3.6 Error-correcting memory controllers traditionally use _____ codes, although some use triple modular redundancy

8.7.3.7 When computer files contain information that is extremely important, a(n) _____ process is used to protect against disasters that might destroy the files

8.7.3.8 The theft of intellectual property has also been an extensive issue for many businesses, especially those in the _____ field

8.7.3.9 _____ usually consists of the destruction of an organization's website, often in an attempt to cause loss of confidence on the part of its customers

9. Networks and Operating Systems

A computer network is a collection of computing devices interconnected by some communication medium. These devices are often referred to as *nodes* of the network.

Every computing *device* needs an operating system (OS) to function, and so does a computer *network*. A **network operating system**, or **network OS**, is system software that controls the various devices on a computer network and facilitates their communication one with each other.

A *network operating system* is a software application that provides a platform for both the functionality of an individual computer and for multiple computers within an interconnected network. Basically, a network operating system controls other software and computer hardware and allows them to run network oriented applications and to share resources through a computer network. The network operating system protects data and establishes communication. Individual computers run client operating systems, while network systems create the software infrastructure necessary for wireless, local and wide area networks to function.

Some of the tasks of a network OS are similar to those of an OS designed for individual computers

memory management and hardware control, for example.

A network OS, however, also has specialized tasks. For example, when network devices, such as printers and disk drives, are used, it is the network OS that will ensure these resources are used correctly and efficiently. Specialized network OS functions also include network security and network administration.

Multiple users will need to access the network simultaneously, and this needs to be managed carefully

All computers ship with operating system software to manage their software and hardware and to provide an interface for humans to use in interacting with the machines. Operating system software is not restricted solely to what we traditionally recognize as *computers*. Smartphones, tablets, network routers and other smart devices also have operating systems.

It is now pretty much expected that any computing device will have the capacity to communicate and interact with other devices, but, in addition, mobile devices (smartphones, tablets, laptops) are expected to be able to connect to communication networks and access the Internet from just about any location where they happen to find themselves. Communication has become an expected capability of the modern computer and any modern operating system is expected to be able to deal with computer networks. **Modern operating systems must be capable of supporting database sharing and application sharing, as well as file and printer access.**

Network operating systems support the basic underlying operating features of networks. These features include support for the various protocols that allow computers to share data. Many network operating systems can automatically detect hardware within the system, and this allows for asset discovery within the network. Network operating systems also support the processing of other software applications that run not only on the individual computers, but also throughout the network.

9.1 Network Topologies

There are many different ways that a computer network can be configured, but almost all will fall into one of three general classifications (topologies):

> bus, star and ring.

Of course any network topology must be supported/implemented by the operating systems on each of the nodes in the network.

9.1.1 Bus Topology

In a network configured with bus topology[xxxii], all of the devices/nodes share access to a common communication medium (the *bus*.)

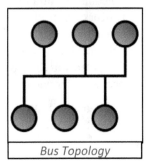

Bus Topology

In a bus network, every node will receive/sense all network communication traffic and it is the responsibility of the operating system of each node to determine whether any given transmission is directed to it and should be acted on, or is intended for some other node and should be ignored.

All nodes on a bus network share the same communication medium. It is quite possible that two of the nodes might attempt to initiate transmission simultaneously, but most communication media do not support simultaneous communication. On networks using these types of media, operating systems must use a media access control technology, such as CSMA/CD[34].

---

[34] Short for *Carrier Sense Multiple Access / Collision Detection,* a set of rules determining how network devices respond when two devices attempt to use a data channel simultaneously (called a *collision.*) Standard Ethernet networks use CSMA/CD to physically monitor the traffic on the line at participating stations. If no transmission is taking place at the time, the particular station can initiate transmission. If two stations attempt to transmit simultaneously, this causes a *collision*, which is detected by all participating stations and all colliding nodes cease transmission. After a random time interval, the stations that collided attempt to transmit again. If another collision occurs, the time intervals from which the random waiting time is selected are increased step by step. This is known as exponential back off. CSMA/CD is a type of *contention* protocol. Networks using the CSMA/CD procedure are simple to implement but do not have deterministic transmission characteristics.

If one is setting up a network, there are a number of reasons that one might choose the bus topology:

- It is quite easy to connect a new computer or peripheral to a bus

- The bus topology is known to work well for small networks

- The operating systems involved are relatively simple, well understood and well documented

- If one node fails, it will (usually) not affect the whole network

On the other hand, the bus topology does have a few disadvantages:

- If implemented using a physical cable (as opposed to wireless communication) the entire network can be shut down by a break in the cable

- The bus topology does not scale well. With a large number of nodes (or just a great deal of network traffic) many collisions are likely to occur, and this will result in slow communications and even, possibly, some information loss.

The simplicity of the bus topology has made it the most popular configuration for home and small business installations, but larger commercial installations are more likely to use a star topology.

As the name implies, the earlier bus network installations used a single physical cable (either coaxial or UTP) connecting all of the nodes. Modern WIFI installations do not have a physical cable connecting the nodes, but they do share a common communication frequency. WIFI network installations do not have the problem of being shut down by a broken cable (although a single malfunctioning node broadcasting continuously would have the same effect) but they do have the same scaling problems. Only one unit can transmit at a time, so an increase in the number of nodes on the network will cause an increase in the collision rate and can result in slower communication.

In a common variant, the nodes share a common communications medium, but avoid collisions by passing "permission to transmit" from node to node. In effect, a logical ring topology implemented on a physical bus network.

Another variant involves a central hub with all peripheral nodes connected to the hub. Any signal from a node is copied by the hub onto the lines connected to all of the other nodes. This could be described as being a logical bus topology with a physical star configuration. These types of installations have, for the most part, been replaced, using switches instead of hubs. (A switch sends signals only to the nodes to which they are directed, rather than to all nodes. This results in a network using a pure star topology.)

9.1.2 Star Topology

In networks with a star topology[xxxiii], there is one central node (or hub) and each of the other (peripheral) nodes is connected only to that central node. Communication between any of the peripheral nodes must be transferred by that central node. All traffic in a star network passes through the central hub which acts as a signal repeater.

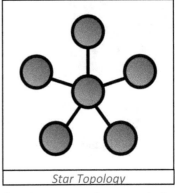

Star Topology

The very earliest networks used a star topology, implemented using a single (mainframe) computer as the central hub and teletype terminals as peripheral nodes. Later, as equipment on peripheral nodes became more sophisticated (personal computers, workstations, smartphones, …) the central hubs became more specialized.

Switches whose only function is to connect peripheral nodes so that they can transfer information. These units support very fast communication but provide few features for monitoring or control.

Routers whose function is to provide communication between nodes on the network, but also with other networks as well.

Database servers that provide large data storage capacities and specialized computation capabilities.

…

The star topology is considered the easiest topology to design and implement. One of its biggest advantages is the ease with which one can add or remove a (peripheral) node.

The fact that all network communications must pass through a central location simplifies the implementation of many security features.

The primary disadvantage of the star topology is that the hub represents a single point of failure. In addition, since all peripheral communication must flow through the central hub, the aggregate central bandwidth can form a network bottleneck for large systems.

9.1.3 Ring Topology

In a ring topology[xxxiv] each node is connected to two other nodes and the collection of node connections forms a closed loop. Data travels around the ring in one direction. When one node sends data to another, the data passes through each intermediate node on the ring until it reaches its destination.

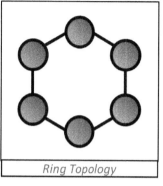

Ring Topology

Ring topology is particularly appropriate for busy networks because it completely avoids collisions between communications and the operating system implementation is relatively simple. On the other hand, information transmission is subject to some delay, since a message will be retransmitted several times before it reaches its intended target. Further, the transmission speed of the network is no faster than that of the slowest link, and, if any node fails, the entire network ceases to function.

9.2 Network Operating System Features

As commented earlier, some of the tasks of a network OS are similar to those of any OS for an individual computer,

> (such as memory management and hardware control)

but a network OS also has specialized tasks.

When network devices are used,

> (printers, disk drives, …)

the network OS must work to ensure these resources are used correctly and efficiently.

Specialized network functions also include network security, network administration and management of multiple users accessing the network.

Most operating systems now found on individual computers have built-in network functions, but operating systems specifically **designed as netw**ork operating systems are common.

> (Linux, Mac OS X Server, Novell and Windows Server are examples.)

A network operating system is the platform on which computer networking operations take place. Basic network features should allow for

file, print and Internet connections

control of data backup and replication.

the management of connective systems for local and wide area networks (LANs and WANs), through configuration and management of routing, switches and other ports.

Again, any modern O/S will contain much built-in software designed to support the networking of computers. Typical O/S software includes an implementation of TCP/IP protocol stack and related utility programs like ping and traceroute. It also includes the necessary device drivers and other software to automatically enable a device's Ethernet or wireless interface. The operating systems of mobile devices normally provide the programs needed to enable Wi-Fi, Bluetooth or other wireless connectivity as well.

Common tasks associated with network operating systems include:

- User administration
- System maintenance activities (like system backup)
- Tasks associated with file management
- Security monitoring on all resources in the network

The features of a network operating system will include:

- Basic operating system features such as:
  - protocol support,
  - processor support,
  - hardware
  - detection and multiprocessing support for applications
- Security features like
  - authentication,
  - restrictions,
  - authorizations
  - and access control
- Features for file management and Web services
- User management features along with provisions for remote management (remote access, permitting remote system management)

9.2.1 System Administration and Maintenance

One of the essential features of a network operating system is that it should have an administrative interface that allows network administrators to monitor and maintain the system. Such an interface would have a menu that allows an administrator to perform functions such as the formatting of hard drives and setting up of security protocols for both the system and individual users. An administrator must be able to configure security and data backup requirements for individual computers as well as for the network as a whole.

Network management can also be used to update software on the individual computers on the network. Rather than having to visit each individual computer for a manual installation, changes can be made directly over the network. This not only allows for automated software updates and installation, but it can also help with maintaining compliance with software licensing

116

9.2.1.1 System Administrators

A **system administrator**, or **sysadmin**, is a person who is responsible for the upkeep, configuration, and reliable operation of computer systems and especially of computers, such as servers, that will be accessed by more than one user. The system administrator seeks to ensure that the uptime, performance, resources, and security of their computers meet the needs of the users, and that they do so within the constraints of a fixed budget.

A network with many users will typically be operated by a specialized (and specially trained) network administrator. The network OS will include sophisticated tools for network management and the administrator must know how to use them. A network administrator must monitor the performance of various parts of the network and should try to address problems before they can have serious impact.

To meet the needs of the users, a system administrator may acquire, install, or upgrade computer components and software; provide routine automation; maintain security policies; troubleshoot; train or supervise staff; or offer technical support for projects.

A network administrator's responsibilities include installing, configuring and supporting an organization's local area network (LAN), wide area network (WAN), Internet systems or a segment of a network system. On-the-job duties such as overseeing network switches, a virtual private network (VPN[35]) and routing are also typical duties.

The tasks that typically constitute the bulk of the administrator's responsibilities would include

- Adding new host machines to the network

- Administering network security

- Administering network services, name services, and electronic mail

- Troubleshooting and repairing network problems

Network administrators are responsible for the implementation, management and troubleshooting of networks. It is their duty to study a company's needs and organize their computer system to satisfy those needs. Network administrators must constantly check data to make sure the system is optimized. They use their data monitoring to look for problems that could be caused, either by the network or by a user. They must also make sure new users have been properly trained in the network usage and must train subordinates on proper uploading and downloading of material that could affect the network.

---

[35] See 9.3.3

9.2.1.1.1 Administration of Users

One of the greatest challenges of managing a network is the managing of the network's users. The people who use the network are much less predictable than the network itself.

Training is a key part of any network manager's job. He/she should try to make sure that everyone who uses the network understands it and knows how to use it.

If the network users don't understand the network, they may unintentionally do all kinds of weird things to it.

One of the system manager's responsibilities should be to make, and maintain, a list summarizing everything that the users need to know about using the network, preferably on one page. Any changes from earlier versions should be highlighted and updated copies should be distributed to all users, regularly.

9.2.2 Security on Network Systems

Network operating systems support many security features that control access to the network. These include authorization and permission for access to the network, with specific control of features such as user management, log-on controls and passwords. Systems also provide access control for features such as remote access and network monitoring.

9.2.2.1 Security Management

The goal of security management is to control access to network resources according to local guidelines so that the network system cannot be damaged (neither unintentionally nor through intentional sabotage.) A security management system will monitor users logging on to a network resource and will refuse access to those who enter inappropriate access codes.

A good security management implementation starts with sound security policies and procedures.

9.2.2.1.1 Authentication

Authentication is the process of identifying users. It usually includes support for:

login and password dialog,

challenge and response,

and messaging.

Authentication is the way a user is identified prior to being allowed access to a resource. There is a fundamental relationship between authentication and authorization. The more authorization privileges a user receives, the stronger the authentication should be.

9.2.2.1.2 Accounting

Accounting capabilities allow for the collecting of information (including security information) used for billing, auditing, and reporting, Information such as:

user identities,

start and stop times,

commands executed

Accounting responsibilities require network managers to track the services that users are accessing as well as how many network resources they are consuming.

9.3 Types of Operating Systems

Corporations, universities, and enterprising individuals have developed hundreds of operating systems over the years. The best-known are those found on personal computers:

- Microsoft Windows
- MacOS
- Linux

Some operating systems are designed for certain types of equipment, such as:

- Apple iOS and Google Android for smartphones and tablets
- Solaris, HP-UX, DG-UX, and other variants of Unix for server computers
- DEC VMS (Virtual Memory System) - for mainframe computers
- Apple's tvOS for Apple TV digital media players
- Wear OS for Google smartwatches

Network operating systems can be separated into two categories:

peer-to-peer network operating systems

client-server operating systems.

Each of these techniques for connecting multiple devices into a single system has its unique advantages:

Client-server operating systems provide flexibility in adding new software and ease of expansion.

Peer to peer systems offer relative the ease of setup and inexpensive operating cost.

Each of the systems also has its disadvantages. These differ notably in dealing with problems (that inevitably occur.):

Client-to-server networks often have a dedicated (but expensive) IT staff to handle the (potentially expensive) problems.

whereas peer-to-peer networks have only each other to solve problems large and small.

9.3.1 Client - Server Networks

The client–server model is a **distributed application** structure that divides tasks or workloads between *providers* of resources or services (called **servers**) and service/resource *requesters* (called **clients.**)

A server **host** runs one or more server programs which share the server's resources with clients.

A *client* does not share resources but instead requests resource(s) and/or service function(s) of server(s).

Clients therefore *initiate* communication sessions with servers.

Servers await incoming requests.

Examples of computer applications that use the client–server model are:

- **Email**,
- **network printing**,
- and the **World Wide Web**

Examples of client-server network operating systems:

- *Novell NetWare*

- *Windows Server*

- *Banyan VINES*

9.3.1.1 Servers

Every individual computer needs its own operating system, and networks also require their own operating systems.

A server is a computer system that provides services over a network.

These services can include things like data storage, file sharing, email management, hosting websites and the like.

Since servers often provide services for large numbers of users, it is important that they carry out their functions quickly so that users are not kept waiting.

In relatively simple networks, one of the regular computers in the network can be used to run the network OS, but in more complicated networks (and especially those with a large number of devices) the network OS resides on a dedicated **computer server,** providing services over the network.

Services of the type mentioned above: data storage, file sharing, email management, hosting websites.

While in principle a regular desktop computer can be configured for use as a server, most servers consist of dedicated machines with hardware components that are specialized and more powerful than those found on normal personal computers.

Systems with multiple servers are often configured in some type of rack, which makes it easier to manage all the hardware, cables and power supplies.

Servers often consume a lot of power and as a result, they are often located in separately cooled environments. These *server rooms* have the additional benefit that they provide additional security.

9.3.1.2 Versatility

One of the greatest strengths of the client-server system is its versatility. It is relatively easy to integrate new technology into client-to-server network connections because the operating system is controlled centrally.

Of course when new technology is integrated into the system the staff and users must be trained to use the technology and this training can be time consuming. There will also inevitably be a few pitfalls as workers integrate the new system into existing protocols.

9.3.2 Peer to Peer Networks

Peer-to-peer (P2P) networking is a method of delivering computer network services in which the participants share a portion of their own resources. (processing power, disk storage, network bandwidth, printing facilities, ...). Such resources are provided directly to other participants without intermediary network hosts or servers. Peer-to-peer network participants are both providers and consumers of network services. This contrasts with more traditional client-server computing.

P2P networks are typically used for connecting nodes via connections that are largely ad hoc. Such networks are useful for many purposes. Sharing content files containing audio, video, data or anything in digital format is very common, and real time data, such as telephony traffic, is also passed using P2P technology.

9.3.2.1 Peer to Peer Networks: Examples

Examples of peer to peer network operating systems:

- *AppleShare*: used for networking connecting Apple products.
- *LANtastic*: supporting DOS, Microsoft Windows, and OS/2 computers
- *Windows for Workgroups*: used for networking peer-to-peer Windows computers.

9.3.2.2 Peer to Peer Networks: Versatility

With respect to "versatility" (as compared to Client-Server networks) peer-to-peer systems depend largely on the existing software platforms installed on computers linked to the network and, while systems for the entire network cannot be changed, each user is able to customize a work station to optimize personal efficiency.

9.3.3   VPN's

For many businesses (and other situations as well) it is not convenient to connect devices with physical cables or with a (local) wireless system.

Offices is buildings separated by great distances, mobile remote representatives and/or salespersons, …

In such situations it is possible to create a *virtual private network* (VPN) by using other, more public, networks (usually the Internet) as a (virtual) communication medium. A VPN, then, is created by establishing a connection over existing networks.

VPN technology was developed to allow remote users and branch offices to access corporate applications and resources. A VPN extends a private network using a public network for communication, and enables users to send and receive data across shared or public networks as if their computing devices were directly connected to the private network. Applications running on a computing device, e.g. a laptop, desktop, smartphone, across a VPN can benefit from the functionality, security, and management of the private network.

VPN users use the same kinds of authentication methods, including passwords or certificates, as are used on any other networks. Communication on a VPN, however, is inherently public, and network security generally requires that all network communication be encrypted. Of course the encryption-decryption process must necessarily interfere with the network communication and slow the "network" communication speed.

9.4   Exercises

9.4.1 One *could* design a wireless network system in which each node would broadcast on its own assigned frequency (and all nodes could receive on all frequencies and distinguish among them all.) In such a system there would be no "collisions". Multiple nodes could transmit simultaneously. What would be some of the advantages and disadvantages of such a system?

9.4.2 Discuss the differences in responsibilities of a sysadmin on a LAN and on a WAN; on a peer to peer versus a client server system, on a corporate, university, small business network and on an individual's home LAN.

9.4.3 Discuss the levels and types of user authentication appropriate for security on peer to peer versus a client server systems, on corporate, university, small business and individuals' home LAN's.

9.4.4 In client-server systems it is normally the client that initiates communication with the server. There are situations in which the server initiates the communication (sometimes described as "push" technology.) Describe some examples where this might be appropriate.

9.4.5 Describe what might be involved in the interface between a network operating system and the individual operating systems of the node devices on a network.

9.4.6 In an office of a small business there might be several computers of the same type and similar configuration. In such a situation would a peer to peer network configuration be more appropriate than client-server? What characteristics of the office environment might make one system preferable to the other?

9.5 Questions

9.5.1 True-False

9.5.1.1 Memory management and hardware control are just two examples of tasks that both kinds of operating systems must deal with

9.5.1.2 There are exactly three different ways that a computer network can be configured. These three general classifications are referred to as topologies.

9.5.1.3 In a bus network, it is quite possible that two of the nodes might attempt to initiate transmission simultaneously. This is usually not a problem, since most communication media will support simultaneous communication.

9.5.1.4 The bus topology does not scale well

9.5.1.5 Some of the tasks of a network OS are similar to those of any OS for an individual computer

9.5.1.6 To meet the needs of the users, a system administrator may acquire, install, or upgrade computer components and software. The training of staff to make use of these, however, is typically the responsibility of the HR department.

9.5.1.7 The more authorization privileges a user receives, the stronger the authentication should be

9.5.1.8 One of the greatest strengths of the client-server system is its versatility

9.5.2 Multiple Choice

9.5.2.1 Individual computers run client operating systems, while network systems create the software infrastructure necessary for _____ networks to function
  a.   wireless
  b.   local
  c.   wide area
  d.   all of the above
  e.   none of the above

9.5.2.2 These features include support for the various _____ that allow computers to share data
  a.   protocols
  b.   tables
  c.   devices
  d.   all of the above
  e.   none of the above

9.5.2.3 To use the _____ network topology, it must be supported/implemented by the operating systems on each of the nodes in the network
    a.   bus
    b.   ring
    c.   star
    d.   all of the above
    e.   none of the above

9.5.2.4 The _____ of the bus topology makes it the most popular configuration for home and small business installations
    a.   low price
    b.   stability
    c.   simplicity
    d.   all of the above
    e.   none of the above

9.5.2.5 In a _____ topology each node is connected to two other nodes
    a.   bus
    b.   ring
    c.   star
    d.   all of the above
    e.   none of the above

9.5.2.6 _____ is an example of a computer application that uses the client-server model
    a.   e-mail
    b.   network printing
    c.   World Wide Web
    d.   all of the above
    e.   none of the above

9.5.2.7 _____ is an example peer to peer operating system
    a.   AppleShare
    b.   LANTastic
    c.   Windows for Workgroups
    d.   all of the above
    e.   none of the above

9.5.3 Completion

9.5.3.1 A computer network is a collection of computing devices interconnected by some communication medium.
    •   These devices are often referred to as _____ of the network

9.5.3.2 The network OS allows the software and hardware to run network oriented applications and to share _____

9.5.3.3 On bus networks operating systems must use a **media** _____ control technology, such as **CSMA/CD**

9.5.3.4 The _____ topology is considered the easiest topology to design and implement

9.5.3.5 In a(n) _____ topology information transmission is subject to some delay, since a message will be retransmitted several times before it reaches its intended target

9.5.3.6 One of the greatest challenges of managing a network is managing the network's

_____

9.5.3.7 _____ responsibilities require network managers to track the services that users are accessing as well as the amount of network resources they are consuming

9.5.3.8 A(n) _____ is a computer system that provides services over a network

10. File Organization and Management

[36]For most users, the file system is one of the most important parts of an operating system.

The primary function of a computer is information processing. The information accumulated and/or created by a user will most often be organized in some kind of *file* and that file will be stored (in binary format) on some kind of storage medium (often disk or tape.)

10.1 Characteristics of Files

Files are collections of information stored on some nonvolatile medium.

Storage on common nonvolatile medium permits the information to be accessed in later work sessions and helps support the sharing of the information between processes.

The file structure is designed to provide a convenient means of data access and information sharing.

In order, then, for a file system to provide the desired functionality, files should:

Have a (reasonably) long term existence

Contain information/data in a form that makes it reasonably accessible.

Be protected from access by unauthorized users/processes.

10.2 File Identification

In order that a user might access information in a file, it is necessary that he/she first identify the file and then identify where in that file the information might be located.

Files are given names as identifiers, but, as storage capacities increased so did the number of files on computing systems, and, users began to have difficulty coming up with unique name for their files. Further, lists of file names started becoming so long that it was difficult to locate a given file from among so many.

Designers began to create file systems in which files could be collected together in groups. They designed systems with [xxxv]*directories*.

A directory, like a file, has a name and can contain things. A directory can contain (any number of) files, but a directory can also contain other directories.

A directory contained in another directory is called a *subdirectory*.

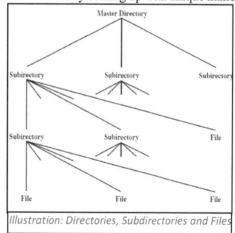

Illustration: Directories, Subdirectories and Files

---

[36] Most of this chapter is taken from *"Operating Systems: Internals and Design Principles"*, by William Stallings (published by Pearson)

This kind of structure allows files with similar characteristics (such as belonging to a specific user) to be grouped together where they can be found more easily. It also simplifies the problem of creating unique names for all files in the system. Any file can be identified using a *complete filename* (full filename, absolute filename) consisting of the "path information" (the sequence of directories and subdirectories containing the file) together with its "relative" filename. Files in different directories can have the same relative file name, but the files in a given directory must have distinct names. A file can be identified (and located) using its absolute file name, although users tend to prefer the much simpler relative file names.

10.3 File Management Systems

The operating system in a computer will provide a file management system to facilitate use of files.

What a file management system should do is:

Provide a means to store data organized as files

Provide a collection of functions that can be performed on files

Support the association of a set of attributes with a file

10.3.1 Basic File Management Operations

Typical file operations that a file management system would provide for users and processes would include:

Create

Delete

Open

Close

Read

Write

10.3.2 Terms Used Concerning File Management

[37]Several terms are frequently used when discussing file management and file operations.

Obviously, there is the term **File**.

A file is a collection of **Records**.

Each record might be made up of one or more **Fields**.

Finally, a collection of files containing interrelated information, might be combined to make up a **Database**.

---

[37] Not all operating systems provide file management systems with the type of structure discussed here. In UNIX and UNIX-like systems, for example, a file is simply a sequence of bytes. Additional structure must be provided by the user processes.

10.3.2.1 Database

A database, as stated above, is a collection of files containing interrelated information.

Example1: A car dealership might store information about their employees in one file, information about the cars available for sale in another file and information about money withheld from employee pay for social security and/or income taxes in a third file

(as well as other files with other information.)

Example 2: A school might store information about students in one file, information about teachers in another file and information about course enrollment in another file.

10.3.2.1.1 Database Operations

Users and processes will make use of the information in the database files. Usually there will be a separate database management system supporting users' interaction with the database, but the DBMS depends on the operating system to support it in providing essential database related operations:

The user/process should be able to:

Retrieve all the records in a file

Retrieve one specific record from a file.

Retrieve the record immediately following the last record retrieved.

Retrieve the record immediately previous to the last record retrieved

Retrieve several records from a file.

Insert a new record into a file

Delete a record from a file.

Modify a record in a file.

10.3.2.2 Record

A record is a collection of related fields that would be treated as a unit.

In Example 1 above, the employee file might be a collection of records, each of which includes a name and a social security number.

Depending on the design, a record may be of fixed length or variable length. This would depend on whether any of the fields have variable length.

It is also possible that a file might have records with only one field (see the previous footnote concerning files in UNIX.) In this case there is no distinction between records and fields.

10.3.2.3 Field

A *field* is a basic element of data, involving a single value. It will typically have a name and will be characterized by its data type.

A field may be of fixed size or variable size (a string, for example.) In the case of variable size data, the actual representation of the data might include a subfield identifying the size/length of the value. (In other situations, the end of the data in the field and or the beginning of a new field might be identified by a special termination/demarcation symbol.)

10.3.2.4 File

As stated above, a file is a collection of information. A file can be referenced by name and is typically structured as a sequence of records, each being similar type.

Files can be created and deleted.

Access control mechanisms can be applied to files, identifying which users and programs can access the file and which cannot[38].

10.3.3 User Requirements for a File Management System

The file management system is ultimately part of the operating system, and, like any other part of the OS, the reason that it is there is to satisfy needs/desires of the users of the system. In the use of the file management system, each user:

should be able to create, delete, read, write and modify files

may have controlled access to other users' files

may control what type of accesses are allowed to his/her files

should be able to move data between files

should be able to back up and recover files in case of damage

should be able to access his or her files by name rather than by numeric identifier

10.3.4 The Objectives of a File Management System

The OS designer, of course, will have a different take on the system than will the end user. From the designer's perspective the file management system should:

Meet the data management needs of the users

Guarantee that the data in the file are valid

Optimize performance

Provide I/O support for a variety of storage device types

Minimize the potential for lost or destroyed data

Provide a standardized set of I/O interface routines to user processes

In the case of multiuser systems, they also provide the necessary multiple user I/O support

---

[38] In some more sophisticated systems, access controls can be applied at the record, or even the field level.

10.4   File Management Software Organization

The complex interactions between users/processes and storage devices is most easily understood (and programmed) as a sequence of [xxxvi]stages.

Elements of File Management

10.4.1   Device Drivers

At the final stage, the lowest level, are the device drivers. This is the software that communicates directly with peripheral devices.

This software is responsible for starting I/O operations on the physical device, and is also responsible for detecting and responding to the completions of the I/O requests.

10.4.2   Basic File System

The *Basic File System* (also referred to as the *physical I/O level*) is the part of the system that deals with where information is stored on secondary storage media.

File System Software Organization

The basic file system:

> deals with blocks (pages, segments) of data that are exchanged with disk (or tape) systems

> is concerned with the placement of blocks/pages/segments on the secondary storage device

> is concerned with buffering blocks in main memory

10.4.3   Basic I/O Supervisor

The I/O supervisor is responsible for all file I/O initiation and termination.

The Basic I/O Supervisor:

> maintains control structures that deal with device I/O, scheduling, and file status

> selects the device on which I/O is to be performed

> is concerned with scheduling disk and tape accesses to optimize performance

> assigns I/O buffers

> allocates secondary memory

131

10.4.4 Logical I/O

The logical I/O stage of the file management process serves as an interface between the "Access Method" stage and the "I/O Supervisor" stage.

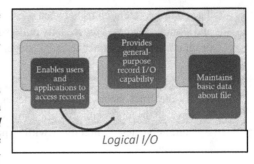

Logical I/O

The "Access Method" stage identifies the part of the file affected (the portion being updated in case of a file *read* operation and the portion whose contents are being copied to secondary storage in case of a file *write* operation)

The "I/O Supervisor" identifies the appropriate data buffer so that the Logical I/O program can copy data to or from the appropriate locations in primary memory.

The "Access Method" stage deals with logical subdivisions of the file. The "I/O Supervisor" stage deals with physical subdivisions related to the data storage.

The "Logical I/O stage converts/translates between the two formats.

10.4.5 Access Method

There are several different ways that a programmer might choose to organize his files.

Among these are:

> indexed,
>
> hashed,
>
> pile,
>
> sequential,
>
> and indexed sequential.

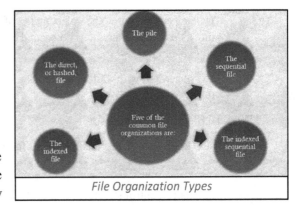

File Organization Types

File organization is the logical structuring of the records controlling the way they can be accessed.

In choosing a file organization, the programmer must consider several factors. Among them are access time, ease of update, economy of storage, ease of maintenance and reliability Which of these factors should have priority will depend on the application that will use the file.

Each access method has some advantages and some disadvantages

10.4.5.1   The Pile

This is the least complicated form of file organization. Data are collected in the order they arrive. Each record consists of one burst of data and records need not have the same length/size. The purpose of the structure is simply to accumulate the mass of data and save it. Records can have different fields, or the same fields in different order Each field in each record must be self describing.

Since there is no structure, record access in a Pile structures file must be by exhaustive search

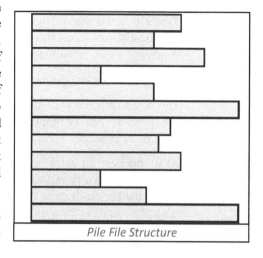

Pile File Structure

This type of file is often used to store collections of data prior to processing. Data can be collected and stored quickly, but later processing will be less efficient and take longer.

10.4.5.2   The Sequential File

This is the most common form of file structure. All records are of the same fixed format, with the same number of fixed length fields in the same order.

Because the length and position of each field is known, only the values need be recorded.

One field (usually the first field and referred to as the *key* field) will be used to identify the record. The key field values for the individual records must be unique

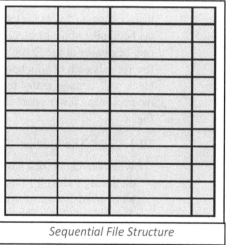

Sequential File Structure

The sequential file structure is especially effective in batch applications and is the only structure that can be used for both tape storage and disk storage.

Sequential file structure does not perform well with applications that do frequent searches, since locating a particular record requires examining a large number of records. The sequential structure is especially inefficient for insertion/deletion operations, since maintaining the sequential structure of the file when inserting or deleting one record requires moving all subsequent records. This is, of course, especially problematic when dealing with large files.

Typically, rather than performing each insertion/deletion to large sequential files, the modifications are stored in a separate *"transaction file"* or *"log file"* (usually with pile structure.) These *"transactions"* are then periodically merged into the main file.

10.4.5.3   The Indexed Sequential File

The access efficiency of the sequential file structure can be improved by the addition of an *index*.

At its simplest, an index is a sequential file in which each record has two fields, one of the key fields from the main data file and a pointer to the record in the main file having that value as the key field. The idea is for index records to identify *blocks* of records in the main file.

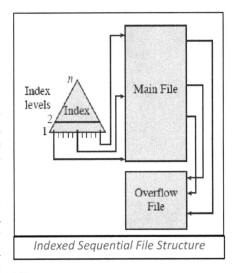

Indexed Sequential File Structure

Using the Indexed Sequential Access Method (ISAM) when one searches for a record in the main file, one begins by searching the index file for the index record having the greatest key value less than or equal to that of the target record. (The pointer from that index record identifies the beginning of the block containing the desired record.) One then searches the main file, beginning at the first record in that block. The index will have (comparatively) few records each of which involves a (relatively) small amount of information. Each block will contain many fewer records than does the main file. Thus the search requires many fewer operations than would the process of searching the entire main file.

10.4.5.3.1   The Indexed Sequential Example: Dictionary

When searching for a word in a dictionary, one typically begins by looking (in the dictionary index) for pages where words begin with the first letter of the desired word (first letters of words serve as key values identifying page numbers in dictionary index.) Then one turns directly to the pages where words begin with the correct letter. From there, one can usually find the target word relatively quickly.

10.4.5.3.2   The Indexed Sequential File: Overflow File

Although the addition of an index improves the efficiency of the search operations in an ISAM file, it does nothing for the problems involved with insertion/deletion operations. In fact, it makes them more difficult because the index file must be modified as well as the main file.

This problem can be addressed by the addition of an *"overflow file"* which functions rather like the *transaction* file used in the sequential file structure.

A pointer field is added to each of the records in the main file. Each record, then, will have a pointer field pointing to the next record in the sequence.

This converts the main file into a linked list.

The records in the main file are initially stored as a physically sequential list, but the linked list structure allows records to be inserted or deleted without moving subsequent records on the main file.

New records are added in the overflow file.

At intervals, of course, the main file will be updated, to incorporate the overflow file into the main file.

Note that while insertion/deletion operations will require updates of the index file, the index file, being much smaller than the main file, can be updated much more easily.

10.4.5.3.3   The Indexed Sequential File: Multiple Indexing Levels

Even greater search efficiency can be obtained using multiple levels of indexing. Especially if the index file is relatively large.

10.4.5.3.3.1   Multiple Indexing Example: Calendar

The key fields for records in a calendar file would naturally include a *year*, a *month* and a *date*.

It would be natural to establish an index file with key fields *year* and *month*. In this index file, each record would include a link to the calendar file identifying the initial record for the first day of the given month and year.

To simplify searching for records in the *year-month* index file, one could then create a second index file in which each record has *year* as the key field and a link to the *January* entry for that year in the *year-month* index file.

With such a structure, the process of accessing a calendar record would begin by searching the second index file for the record for the appropriate year (12 times faster than searching in the *year-month* index file.) The link from that record in the second index file identifies a record in the *year-month* index file. One can search from that record and find the appropriate year-month record in no more than 12 operations, and from that link, find the first record for that year-month combination in the main calendar.

10.4.5.4   The Indexed File

Using the indexed sequential structure, one is basically limited (by the index) as to the way records can be accessed.

The dictionary structure (see 10.4.5.3.1) supports searches based on spelling but provides little support for a search based on the occurrence of a particular letter within words, or for a search based on word size

The calendar structure (see 10.4.5.3.3.1) supports access based on dates but provides little support for a search based on holidays or days of the week.

In some applications, flexibility in the attributes for searches is desirable. In such situations, this kind of flexibility can be provided by the use of multiple index files using keys from different fields in the main file. When using an indexed file structure, we do not assume, as we do with the ISAM structure, that the main file is structured as a list. The index files are lists and all file access operations are done using one of them.

Indexed File

It is also assumed that each record in the main file is referenced by at least one record in one of the index files and, so, the records in the main file need not be of uniform size.

Indexed files are used in applications where timeliness of information is important. Although they support quick efficient access to information, they introduce extra complications (and time) in insertion/deletion operations, since (possibly multiple) index file(s) must be updated as well as the main data file.

With this kind of structure there are two possible kinds of index files:

Exhaustive Index files: Each record in the main file is referenced by a record in the index file. (It is preferable that at least one index file be exhaustive. If no, then the requirement that each entry be referenced by at least one index becomes difficult to enforce.)

Partial index files: Some records in the main file are not referenced by records in the index.

10.4.5.4.1 Indexed File Example: Personnel File

In the personnel file for a large company, one of the fields of the record for each employee would certainly be his/her social security number, and so the social security number could be used as the key for an exhaustive index for the personnel file.

Many (but certainly not all) of the employees might be classified as "supervisory personnel" and a list of these employees might be used as a partial index.

10.4.5.5 The Hashed (Direct) File

In situations which require very quick access (and where storage space is available) the *direct* or *hashed* file structure might be used.

For this structure, records must have a fixed size and each record must have a unique key field (or combination of fields functioning together as a key.) The system uses a function ("hash" function) to calculate a number (based on the value in the key field.)

The number calculated by the hash function will be the offset in the main file where the data record will be stored/found[39].

File access is quite efficient and, since the system does not assume that records will be stored sequentially, insertion/deletion operations can also be carried out very quickly.

10.5   File Sharing

In a multiuser system, it is always necessary to deal with the problem of how to share files between users.

The sharing of files among users raises two kinds of issues: those of access rights and those created by the possibility of simultaneous access.

10.5.1   Access Rights

If different users have access to a given file, it is reasonable that not all of them would have the same *kinds* of access rights, and it is the file management system that must enforce the rules governing these different types of accesses.

Over the years, a wide range of rights have been used in the different operating systems. The following is a typical collection of the rights that might be assigned to a user for a given file.

None the user would not even be allowed to read the user directory that includes the file

Knowledge the user can determine that the file exists and who its owner is. He/she might then petition the owner for additional access rights

Execution the user can load and execute a program but cannot copy it

Reading the user can read the file for any purpose, including copying it and/or executing it

Appending the user can add data to the file but cannot modify or delete any of the file's existing contents

Updating the user can modify, delete, and add to the file's data

Changing protection the user can change the access rights granted to other users

Deletion the user can delete the file from the file system

Normally one user will be designated as a file's "owner" (usually the person who created the file.) The owner will typically have all of the rights listed above.

---

[39] In the event that the hash function calculates the same value for different records (with different key values) the records with duplicate hash values will be stored in an overflow file provided by the system.

Access can be granted to different *classes* of users:

Owner: usually the initial creator of the file, and has full rights. He/she may grant rights to others

Specific Users: individual users who are designated by user ID

User Groups: a set of users who are not individually defined

All: all users who have access to this system. These are known as *public* files

10.5.2 Simultaneous Access

When modification access (append, update) is given to more than one user, then the file management system has the responsibility of enforcing some kind of discipline to avoid the kinds of mutual access problems described in chapter 4.

10.6 Record Blocking

The structure of a file will be dictated by several factors:

the logic of the data representation,

the kinds of data being represented

the types of access that will be required by the type of application for which it is to be used.

The file *storage*, however, is dictated by the structure of the disk storage system.

Where the application software sees the file as a collection of records, whose structures are designed by the programmer, the disk storage system sees the file as a collection of fixed size "blocks" (often called *pages*, sometimes *segments*) whose size and structure are controlled by considerations such as sector size and cluster size.

If a file is to be stored on a disk, the records must be distributed in groups of blocks, corresponding to sections of disk where the data will be stored. This process of grouping the records into blocks is, of course, called "blocking"

There are three ways that blocking can be carried out:

1) *Fixed-Length Blocking* – fixed length records are used, and an integral number of records are stored in a block

2) *Variable-Length Spanned Blocking* – variable-length records are used and are packed into blocks with no unused space

3) *Variable-Length Unspanned Blocking* – variable-length records are used, but spanning is not employed

10.6.1 Fixed-Length Blocking

If the file has fixed length records, then every block can contain the same number of records. With fixed length blocking, each record is contained entirely in one block. It is likely that the records will not occupy all of the space in a block, so there will be a small amount of unused space (waste space) in each block.

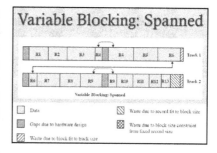

This is the most common mode for sequential files with fixed length records.

10.6.2 Variable-Length Spanned Blocking

With variable length records, some systems will fill each block, storing records end to end, and dividing some records between two blocks (storing the record "spanning" the gap between the blocks.) This system avoids wasted storage space but is difficult to implement. Records that span two blocks would require two I/O operations. Files will be difficult to update.

10.6.3 Variable-Length Unspanned Blocking

With variable length records, some systems will fill each block, storing records end to end, but will not divide records between blocks. With this kind of system, there will be some wasted space at the end of each block if the next record is too large to fit in the remaining unused space. Records are limited to the size of a block.

10.7 Secondary Storage Management

When the records of a file have been assigned to blocks, the file management system must then determine where each of the blocks will be stored in the secondary storage. The system must in fact do two things:

It must keep track of which locations in secondary storage are assigned to which blocks allocated to which files.

It must keep track of which locations in secondary storage are not so assigned and are available for allocation.

There are several issues involved in allocation of disk blocks to files:

1. When a new file is created, will the maximum space required be allocated all at once or *dynamically* as needed?

2. Space will be allocated to a file in sections of contiguous space (called portions.) What size is appropriate for "portions"?

3. What sort of data structure would be used to keep track of the portions assigned to a file?

10.7.1 *Preallocation* versus *Dynamic Allocation*

A *preallocation* policy requires that the maximum size of a file be declared at the time of the file creation request. Unfortunately, for many applications it is difficult to estimate reliably the maximum potential size of the file. For such applications, preallocation tends to be wasteful because users and application programmers tend to overestimate size, since they want to avoid running out of space.

Dynamic allocation allocates portions to a file as/when they are needed.

Clearly, if it is possible to preidentify the size of a file, then preallocation is more efficient, but in the case of a file whose size cannot be reliably estimated, dynamic allocation supports much more efficient use of storage space.

10.7.2 Portion Size

In choosing a portion size there is a trade-off between efficiency from the point of view of a single file versus overall system efficiency.

Things to take into consideration:

1) contiguity of space increases performance, particularly for Retrieve_Next operations, and especially for transactions running in a transaction-oriented operating system

2) having larger number of (smaller) portions will increase the size of tables needed to manage the allocation information

3) having fixed-size portions simplifies the reallocation of space

4) having variable-size or small fixed-size portions minimizes waste of unused storage due to overallocation

These factors interact, and the primary alternatives are:

Large variable contiguous portions: Variable size avoids waste and large size results in small file allocation tables. Variable size allocation, however, has the potential to result in fragmentation.

Blocks: Small fixed portions result in great flexibility and avoids fragmentation, but results in large file allocation tables and longer search times during allocation.

10.7.3 Data Structure for Portions Assigned to Files

There are three commonly used methods for keeping track of which portions/blocks are assigned to which files: contiguous allocation, chained allocation and indexed allocation

10.7.3.1 Contiguous Allocation

[xxxvii]This system can only be used with a preallocation policy. A single contiguous set of blocks is allocated to a file at the time of file creation.

It is the best from the point of view of the individual sequential file, but is subject to external fragmentation which could make it difficult to find space for a new file.

Contiguous File Allocation

The file allocation table only needs a single entry for each file, showing the starting block and the length of the file.

Supports random access, since it is easy to calculate the location (on disk) of any given block.

10.7.3.2 Chained Allocation

[xxxviii]Allocation is on a block by block basis and each block includes a pointer to the next block. This system is typically used to support a dynamic allocation policy.

Since blocks are allocated individually, there is no fragmentation. The file allocation table entry for each file requires only the starting block, although, for purposes of efficiency, it

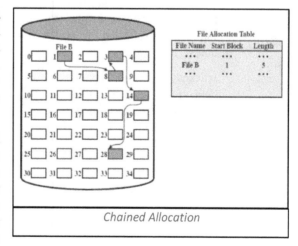

Chained Allocation

will normally also include the file length and/or the final block.

This organization does not support random access. It is best suited to files that will be processed sequentially.

Neither does this system support the principle of locality, since there is no reason for sequential blocks to be located physically near each other. To alleviate this problem, many systems periodically [xxxix]consolidate files.

Chained Allocation after Consolidation

10.7.3.3 Indexed Allocation

With this system there is a separate index for each file. Each index has an entry for each portion allocated to the file.

Portions may be [xl]fixed size blocks (which eliminates fragmentation) or [xli]variable size (which improves locality.) In either case, files can be consolidated from time to time.

Indexed allocation supports both sequential and random access. It is the most popular form of allocation.

Indexed Allocation with Block Portions

Indexed Allocation with Variable Length Portions

10.7.4   Free Space Management

Just as allocated space must be managed, so must the unallocated space. To perform file allocation, it is necessary to know which blocks are *available* for allocation. A number of techniques have been used to keep track of available space. Among the most popular are:

Bit Tables, Chained Free Portions, Indexing, and Free Block List.

10.7.4.1   Bit Tables

This technique uses a vector with a bit for each block on the disk. An entry of 0 indicates that the block is available for allocation and an entry of 1 indicates that the block is allocated to a file.

This is memory efficient, being as small as possible. It also makes it relatively easy to locate groups of contiguous free blocks. However, although it is as small as possible, a bit table can be quite large, and, thus, searching one can be time consuming. Most operating systems that use bit tables maintain auxiliary data structures summarizing the contents of subranges of the bit table.

10.7.4.2   Chained Free Portions

The free portions can be linked together, each free portion having a link to the next (and, in the case of variable size portions, the length of the portion.)

This method has no space overhead, since there is no need for an allocation table, only a pointer to the first free portion, and all of the pointers are within the unallocated portions and take up no (allocated) space.

With this method, free space is subject to fragmentation. With variable sized portions, creation of files can be time consuming since each portion requires a search of the linked list until a big enough space is found. Similarly, deleting fragmented files can also be time consuming.

10.7.4.3   Indexing

The indexing approach treats the free space as an indexed sequential file. Each free portion has an entry in the index table.

10.7.4.4   Free Block List

With this method, each block is assigned a number, and a list of the free blocks is maintained. This list (index) will typically be too long to keep in main memory but will be maintained as a file on disk. As a disk file it occupies a very small proportion of the space.

The block list can be structured as either:

A **stack**: A part (the most recently added part) in main memory. When a block is to be newly allocated, it will be popped from the top of the stack, which will be kept in main memory. When a block is deallocated, it will be pushed onto the stack. Either operation is performed in main memory and, thus, takes very little time.

A **FIFO Queue**: Both ends of the queue would be in main memory. When a block is newly allocated, it will be removed from the front of the queue and when a block is deallocated, it will be added to the back of the queue. Again, either operation will be quite fast, as it will involve only main memory, and not disk operations.

In either of these situations, a background thread can run, moving list entries to or from disk to maintain optimum sizes for the main memory sections of the lists and adjusting locations of blocks within the main list to facilitate contiguity.

10.8 Exercises

10.8.1 Will the wider use of SSD devices for secondary storage have any long term effect on the accepted methods of file structures and file storage?

10.8.2 In some systems (UNIX and UNIX-like systems, for example) a file is simply a sequence of bytes. What are the advantages and disadvantages of such a system?

10.8.3 In choosing a file organization, the programmer must consider several factors. Among them are access time, ease of update, economy of storage, ease of maintenance and reliability Which of these factors should have priority will depend on the application that will use the file. What are some of the kinds of applications that would give higher priorities to each of these?

10.9 Questions

10.9.1 True-False

10.9.1.1 Files are collections of information stored on disk or other nonvolatile medium.

10.9.1.2 In UNIX and UNIX-like systems a file is simply a sequence of bytes. Additional structure, such as that described in the text, must be provided by the user processes

10.9.1.3 A record must be of fixed length

10.9.1.4 A field is a basic element of data, involving a single value. It must, therefore be of fixed size.

10.9.1.5 In some sophisticated systems, access controls can be applied at the record, or even the field level

10.9.1.6 In the use of the file management system, each user may have controlled access to other users' files

10.9.1.7 There are several different ways that a programmer might choose to organize his files

10.9.1.8 In choosing a file organization, the programmer must consider several factors. Among them are access time, ease of update, economy of storage, ease of maintenance and reliability These factors will generally have about equal priority, but can be have different effects in different applications

10.9.1.9 Sequential file structure does not perform well with applications that do frequent searches

10.9.1.10 In some applications, flexibility in the attributes for searches is desirable. In such situations, such flexibility can be provided by the use of multiple levels of indexing.

10.9.1.11 Although they support quick efficient access to information, multiple index files introduce extra complications (and time) in insertion/deletion operations

10.9.1.12 The different operating systems have consistently used the same set of file access rights

10.9.1.13 A number of techniques have been used to keep track of disk space available for allocation.

10.9.2 Multiple Choice

10.9.2.1 In order for a file system to provide the desired functionality, files should:

_____
a. Have a (reasonably) long term existence
b. Contain information/data in a form that makes it reasonably accessible.
c. Be protected from access by unauthorized users/processes
d. all of the above
e. none of the above

10.9.2.2 If a directory is contained in another directory, it is called a(n) _____ directory
a. inner
b. lower
c. sub
d. all of the above
e. none of the above

10.9.2.3 _____ is/are responsible for starting I/O operations on the physical device
a. Device Drivers
b. Basic file system
c. Basic I/O supervisor
d. Logical I/O
e. none of the above

10.9.2.4 _____ is/are concerned with buffering blocks in main memory
- a. Device Drivers
- b. Basic file system
- c. Basic I/O supervisor
- d. Logical I/O
- e. none of the above

10.9.2.5 _____ select(s) the device on which I/O is to be performed
- a. Device Drivers
- b. Basic file system
- c. Basic I/O supervisor
- d. Logical I/O
- e. none of the above

10.9.2.6 The _____ is the least complicated form of file organization
- a. pile
- b. sequential file
- c. indexed sequential file
- d. indexed file
- e. none of the above

10.9.2.7 The _____ is the most common form of file structure
- a. pile
- b. sequential file
- c. indexed sequential file
- d. indexed file
- e. none of the above

10.9.2.8 ISAM stands for _____
- a. Indexed Sequential Access Marking
- b. Insertion Sequential Access Marking
- c. Indexed Sequential Access Method
- d. Insertion Sequential Access Method
- e. none of the above

10.9.2.9 With the hashed file structure,
- a. data access is efficient and insertion/deletion operations can be carried out very quickly
- b. insertion/deletion operations can be carried out very quickly, although data access can be inefficient
- c. data access is efficient but insertion/deletion operations can be a little slow
- d. data access can be inefficient and insertion/deletion operations are somewhat slow
- e. none of the above

10.9.2.10 The structure of a file as a collection of records is dictated by _____
- a. the logic of the data representation
- b. the kinds of data being represented
- c. the types of access that will be required by the type of application for which it is to be use
- d. all of the above
- e. none of the above

146

10.9.2.11 The _____ blocking system avoids wasted storage space but is difficult to
implement
   a. fixed length
   b. fixed length unspanned
   c. variable length spanned
   d. variable length unspanned
   e. none of the above

10.9.2.12 Smaller portion sizes will result in:
   a. larger allocation tables and larger amounts of wasted storage space
   b. larger allocation tables and smaller amounts of wasted storage space
   c. smaller allocation tables and larger amounts of wasted storage space
   d. smaller allocation tables and smaller amounts of wasted storage space
   e. none of the above

10.9.2.13 _____ allocation is the most popular form of allocation
   a. contiguous
   b. chained
   c. indexed
   d. all of the above are about equally popular
   e. none of the above

10.9.2.14 With the _____ method for tracking available space, the free space is
subject to fragmentation.
   a. bit tables
   b. chained free portions
   c. indexed
   d. all of the above
   e. none of the above

10.9.3 Completion

10.9.3.1 For most users, the _____ system is one of the most important parts of an
operating system

10.9.3.2 Each record might be made up of one or more _____

10.9.3.3 A(n) _____ is a collection of related fields that would be treated as a unit

10.9.3.4 In sequential files, one field (usually the first field and referred to as the ____
field) will be used to identify the record

10.9.3.5 Although the addition of an index improves the efficiency of the search
operations in an ISAM file, it does nothing for the problems involved with
insertion/deletion operations. This problem is addressed by the addition of a(n)
"_____ file"

10.9.3.6 In the case of a file whose size cannot be reliably estimated, _____
allocation supports efficient use of storage space

Answers to Odd Numbered Chapter Questions

1.4 Chapter 1 Questions:

1.4.1 True-False

1.4.1.1 The primary function of a computing system is to process data.

Ans: T

1.4.1.3 Operating Systems are among the most complex pieces of software ever developed

Ans: T

1.4.1.5 On the earliest computers there was nothing even remotely resembling what we would call an operating system

Abs: T

1.4.1.7 "compute bound" programs (programs that seldom stop to wait for I/O) tend to block the progress of other programs in systems without time slicing.

Ans: T

1.4.1.9 The 1960's saw a segmentation of the computer market as less complex and less expensive computers (minicomputers) entered the market. This division of the market had an immediate impact on operating system development

Ans: F "compute bound" programs (programs that seldom stop to wait for I/O) tend to block the progress of other programs in systems without time slicing.

1.4.1.11 With the arrival, and wide public acceptance of the smart phone (a combination of cell phone and computer) manufacturers were able to use simpler user interfaces since few of the phones were being used for complex programming tasks

Ans: F With the arrival, and wide public acceptance of the smart phone (a combination of cell phone and computer) came the need for different and even more sophisticated user interfaces

1.4.1.13 An embedded system's key feature is dedication to specific functions, and for this reason they normally require specialized processors.

Ans: F An embedded system's key feature is dedication to specific functions, but they often require strong general-purpose processors.

1.4.2 Multiple Choice

1.4.2.1 The operating system is an important part of the software of any computer system. An operating system has several functions. One of these functions would be:
a.   controlling access to the processor(s)
b.   providing a set of services to users of the system (determining how they can interact with the system)
c.   managing system hardware components
d.   all of the above
e.   none of the above

1.4.2.3 The first primitive operating systems, which were developed in the mid-_____ were small supervisor programs that provided basic I/O operations (such as control of punch card and/or tape readers and printers.)
a.   1940s
b.   1950s
c.   1960s
d.   1970s
e.   none of the above

1.4.2.5 The 1960's saw a segmentation of the computer market as less complex and less expensive computers (_____) entered the market.
a.   minicomputers
b.   personal computers
c.   microcomputers
d.   smartphones
e.   none of the above

1.4.3 Completion

1.4.3.1 A processing unit (also referred to as a _____) controls the operation of the computer and performs the data processing functions. It executes the commands that result in the processing of the system's data.

Ans: CPU

1.4.3.3 The operating system's I/O _____ provide control of movement of data between the computer and external environments, including: storage devices, communications equipment and other I/O devices

Ans: modules

1.4.3.5 The first primitive operating systems, which were developed in the mid-1950s were small *supervisor programs* that provided basic I/O operations (such as control of punch card and/or tape readers and printers.) The systems using these were described as _____ processing systems.

Ans: batch

1.4.3.7 A process contains three components: *executable code, the associated data* needed by the process and the *execution* _____ (or "process state") of the program.

Ans: context

1.4.3.9 It was not cost effective to build computers in which the high speed technology was used for *all* of the RAM, but it *was* possible to include a relatively small amount of high speed RAM (called a (n) _____)

Ans: cache

1.4.3.11 As personal computers became larger and faster, more complex interface systems (_____'s) were developed that made the personal computer easier for untrained people to use

Ans: GUI

2.3 Chapter 2 Questions

2.4.1 True-False

2.4.1.1 Because of the limited memory available, operating systems used on small devices are necessarily quite complex.

Ans: F   Operating systems used on small devices may be relatively simple

2.4.1.3 The critical code of the kernel is usually loaded into a separate area of memory, which is protected from access by application programs or other, less critical parts of the operating system.

Ans: T

2.4.1.5 The monolithic model differs from other operating system architectures in that it alone defines a high-level virtual interface over computer hardware.

Ans: T

2.4.1.7 Among the factors that must be considered in the design of resource allocation policies are: fairness, differential responsiveness and efficiency. Resources should also be allocated in a manner that avoids "deadlocks" and "starvation". These objectives are not necessarily mutually consistent

Ans; T

2.4.2 Multiple Choice

2.4.2.1 A computing system requires a set of resources for the _____ of data
   a.   processing
   b.   moving
   c.   storing
   d.   all of the above
   e.   none of the above

2.4.2.3 Most modern computing systems are _____ systems
    a.   batch
    b.   application
    c.   multiprocessing
    d.   multiuser
    e.   none of the above

2.4.3 Completion

2.4.3.1 A computing system requires a set of _____ for the processing, moving and storing of data

Ans: resources

2.4.3.3 The _____ is a computer program that is the core of a computer's operating system, with complete control over everything in the system.

Ans: kernel

2.4.3.5 A(n) _____ **kernel** is an operating system architecture in which the entire operating system is working in "kernel space" and is alone in supervisor mode

Ans: monolithic

2.4.3.7 Application programs are (generally) resource *users*. The operating system, on the other hand, functions as the resource _____

Ans: manager

3.5 Chapter 3 Questions

3.5.1 True-False

3.5.1.1 One of the disadvantages of dynamically loadable modules is their relatively large I/O overhead when compared to building all conceivable functionality into the operating system image.

Ans: F Dynamically loadable modules incur a small overhead when compared to building all conceivable functionality into the operating system image.

3.5.1.3 The OS maintains all PCBs in the **Process Scheduling Queue (PSQ).**

Ans:F The OS maintains all PCBs in Process Scheduling Queues. The system will maintain a separate queue for each of the process states and PCBs of all processes in the same execution state are placed in the same queue.

3.5.1.5 There are several types of I/O module

Ans: T

3.5.1.7 Communication with the external environment will generally use the same data buses that are used in the execution of normal programs

Ans: T

3.5.1.9   Data transmission and storage usually incorporate some kind of error detection strategies to identify when and (if possible) what kinds errors have occurred, either in storage or transmission. These detection strategies often involve parity bits

Ans: T

3.5.2   Multiple Choice

3.5.2.1   Using dynamically loadable modules _____
   a.   helps to keep the amount of code running in kernel space to a minimum.
   b.   will reduce operating system footprint to optimum size
   c.   allows for easy extension/upgrading of the operating system
   d.   all of the above
   e.   none of the above

3.5.2.3   Possibly the most commonly used state model is the _____ model
   a.   one state
   b.   two state
   c.   five state
   d.   seven state
   e.   none of the above

3.5.2.5   In systems with cache memory and/or virtual memory, the memory manager will typically set up _____ to keep track of which sections of memory are allocated to which processes, which are associated with sections of cache and which processes involve what kind of sections of virtual memory.
   a.   lists
   b.   queues
   c.   tables
   d.   stacks
   e.   none of the above

3.5.2.7   A hardware system that might use DMA would be a _____
   a.   disk drive controller
   b.   sound card
   c.   network card
   d.   all of the above
   e.   none of the above

3.5.3   Completion

3.5.3.1   Division of the system into dynamically loadable _____ is a very flexible way of handling an operating system image at runtime (as opposed to rebooting with a different operating system image whenever additional functionality might be required.)

Ans: modules

3.5.3.3   A process is a unit of activity characterized by having a single sequential thread of execution, a current state, and an associated set of system _____

Ans: resources

3.5.3.5   In a five (or seven) state model system, a process is said to be in the _____ state if it is in memory and is in the "waiting" queue, waiting to be assigned to a processor to be executed

Ans: Ready

3.5.3.7   For the degree of _____ to be stable, the average rate of process creation must be equal to the average departure rate of processes leaving the system

Ans: multiprogramming

3.5.3.9   DMA is an acronym for _____ *Memory Access*

Ans: Direct

4.5   Chapter 4 Questions

4.5.1   True-False

4.5.1.1   All modern operating systems have to deal with the problems of concurrent processes (processes dealing with things that are going on simultaneously.)

Ans: T

4.5.1.3   There is a unique mechanism which has been developed to implement critical regions.

Ans: F Several mechanisms have been developed to implement critical regions.

4.5.1.5   Dynamic resource sharing tends to decrease the chance of deadlocks.

Ans: F   Dynamic resource sharing *increases* the chance of deadlocks.

4.5.1.7   Most current operating systems cannot prevent deadlocks

Ans: T

4.5.2   Multiple Choice

4.5.2.1   The common element of all (successful) synchronization schemes is that of a _____ whose execution must be handled as a unit without being interleaved with the execution of others.
a.   *critical region*
b.   *hot area*
c.   *singular section*
d.   *controlling process*
e.   none of the above

4.5.3   Completion

4.5.3.1   All modern operating systems have to deal with the problems of _____ processes (processes dealing with things that are going on simultaneously.)

Ans: concurrent

4.5.3.3 Concurrency creates the possibility of _____ and/or starvation

Ans: deadlock

4.5.3.5 The _____ instruction is an instruction used to write the value 1 to a memory location ("set" the memory location) and return its old value as a single atomic (i.e., non-interruptible) operation

Ans: test-and-set

4.5.3.7 _____ is a name traditionally assigned to a semaphore used for mutual exclusion

Ans: Mutex

4.5.3.9 _____ is the name given to indefinite postponement of process because it requires some resources before it can run but the resource(s) is/are never allocated to this process, usually because the necessary resource(s) is/are widely used, and the system tends to have numerous higher priority processes making use of it/them.

Ans: Starvation

5.4 Chapter 5 Questions

5.4.1 True-False

5.4.1.1 Since most modern computing systems have several processors, it is rare for the operating systems to have to deal with situations involving more jobs/processes than there are processors

Ans: F Although most modern computing systems have several processors, the operating systems will typically deal with situations involving more jobs/processes than there are processors

5.4.1.3 A device running at 100 percent CPU utilization would be very quick to respond to management or system events.

Ans: F A device running at 100 percent CPU utilization might be slow to respond to management or system events.

5.4.2 Multiple Choice

5.4.2.1 To _____ a system would prioritize I/O bound (interactive) processes, and use short time slices to maximize the number of processes working toward the point where they need user interaction. Compute bound processes would obviously suffer from this system
a.   **minimize *response time***
b.   maximize *cpu efficiency*
c.   prioritize *fairness*
d.   prioritize *capacity*
e.   none of the above

5.4.2.3   There are a number of algorithms used by systems for CPU allocation. One of these ____ is the simplest, but was only used on the earliest batch processing systems
   a.   **FIFO**
   b.   SJF
   c.   HRRN
   d.   FPPS
   e.   none of the above

5.4.2.5   There are a number of algorithms used by systems for CPU allocation. One of these ____ places processes in a queue ordered by estimated processing time remaining
   a.   EDF
   b.   **SRT**
   c.   RR
   d.   PS
   e.   none of the above

5.4.3   Completion

5.4.3.1   In a(n) _____ system, a process, once it is given access to a processor, will be allowed to continue using that processor until it relinquishes control

Ans: non-preemptive

5.4.3.3   PS is one of the most common scheduling systems in _____ systems.

Ans: batch

6.8   Chapter 6 Questions

6.8.1   True-False

6.8.1.1   RAM is much cheaper than external storage

Ans: F External storage is much cheaper than RAM

6.8.1.3   The CPU can only deal directly with locations in primary storage.

Ans: T

6.8.1.5   Locality of reference has strengthened for user software. This is mostly attributed to the spread of object-oriented programming techniques that emphasize unified structures.

Ans: F Locality of reference has *weakened* for user software. This is mostly attributed to the spread of object-oriented programming techniques that favor large numbers of small functions and the use of sophisticated data structures like trees and hash tables that tend to result in chaotic memory reference patterns

6.8.1.7   Pages usually correspond to natural divisions of a program such as individual routines or data tables, so paging is generally more visible to the programmer than segmentation.

Ans: F Segments usually correspond to natural divisions of a program such as individual routines or data tables, so segmentation is generally more visible to the programmer than paging

6.8.1.9 Virtual memory systems using segmentation will be much less subject to thrashing than will paging systems.

Ans: T

6.8.2   Multiple Choice

6.8.2.1   Virtual memory systems are subject to _____, which occurs when the computer's virtual memory resources become saturated, leading to a constant state of exchanging data in memory for data on disk,
a.   whiplash
b.   thrashing
c.   rocking
d.   bouncing
e.   none of the above

6.8.2.3   The replacement policy decides where in the cache a copy of a particular entry of main memory will go. If the replacement policy is free to choose any entry in the cache to hold the copy, the cache is called _____ *associative.*
a.   *completely*
b.   *totally*
c.   *fully*
d.   *entirely*
e.   none of the above

6.8.3   Completion

6.8.3.1   Systems can use disk space as an extension of their memory space (_____ memory systems)

Ans: virtual

6.8.3.3   The time it takes for the desired sector to rotate to a position under the read/write head is called rotational _____

Ans: latency

6.8.3.5 There are a number of possible strategies for choosing a page to swap out. With one of them, _____ page references closer to the current time have more impact than earlier page references. This ensures that pages referenced more recently, even though less frequently, will have higher priority over pages frequently referenced in the past

Ans: aging

6.8.3.7 It is not cost effective to build computers in which all of the RAM is of high speed technology, but it is possible to include a relatively small section using high speed RAM (such a section is called a _____.)

Ans: cache

7.9 Chapter 7 Questions

7.9.1 True-False

7.9.1.1 The size of the byte has historically been hardware dependent and no definitive standards existed that mandated the size

Ans: T

7.9.1.3 RAID 0 systems require twice as many disks as do RAID 1 systems to achieve the same storage capacity

Ans: F RAID 1 systems require twice as many disks as do RAID 0 systems to achieve the same storage capacity

7.9.2 Multiple Choice

7.9.2.1 A *word* is a fixed-sized piece of data handled as a unit by the instruction set or the hardware of the processor. The number of bits in a word (the word _____) is an important characteristic of any specific processor design or computer architecture
    a.   size
    b.   width
    c.   length
    d.   any of the above
    e.   none of the above

7.9.2.3 RAID _____ provides good performance of reads, but the performance doing writes is low because of the need to write all parity data to a single disk
    a.   0
    b.   1
    c.   4
    d.   5
    e.   none of the above

7.9.3 Completion

7.9.3.1 Computers are _____ devices and information is represented in binary format

Ans: digital

7.9.3.3 In computing, a(n) _____ is the natural unit of data used by a particular processor design.

Ans: word

7.9.3.5 When the processor needs to read or write a location in main memory, it first checks for a corresponding entry in the cache. The cache checks for the contents of the requested memory location in any cache lines that might contain that address. If the processor finds that the memory location is in the cache, a cache _____ has occurred. In this case, the processor immediately reads or writes the data in the cache line

Ans: hit

7.9.3.7 On some platforms the file format is dictated by its filename _____

Ans: extension

8.7 Chapter 8 Questions

8.7.1 True-False

8.7.1.1 By computer security, we basically mean the maintenance of system integrity and the availability and confidentiality of information dealt with by the computer system. The operating system plays a paramount role in the overall security of the system.

Ans: T

8.7.1.3 Systems have recently begun using error detection and correction codes to improve the reliability of data storage media.

Ans: F Error detection and correction codes are often used to improve the reliability of data storage media. This is **not** a *recent* development. In fact, a "parity track" was present on the first magnetic tape data storage in 1951.)

8.7.1.5 Operating systems usually have reporting facilities that are used to provide notifications when errors are transparently recovered.

Ans: T

8.7.1.7 Frequent password changes ensure that legacy accounts do not become weak points in the system.

Ans: T

8.7.2 Multiple Choice

8.7.2.1 One of the functions of an operating system is to provide a level of security, and so, the system should work to defend against _____
a. physical malfunctions
b. user errors
c. attacks from external sources
d. all of the above
e. none of the above

8.7.2.3 According to a 2013 report 95 percent of advanced and targeted attacks involved spear-phishing scams with emails containing malicious attachments that can cause malware to be downloaded onto the user's computing device. report in 2014 showed that this proportion had fallen to _____ percent.
a. 91
b. 78
c. 44
d. 22
e. none of the above

8.7.3 Completion

8.7.3.1 Data errors in a digital system can be due to manufacturing defects, wear, environmental _____, and many other factors.

Ans: EMF

8.7.3.3 A(n) _____ of a collection (of a fixed word length) of data is a modular arithmetic sum of that data.

Ans: checksum

8.7.3.5 (also known as resyncing, rebuilding, or reconstructing) is the process of repairing a damaged device using the contents of healthy devices.

Ans: Resilvering

8.7.3.7 When computer files contain information that is extremely important, a(n) _____ process is used to protect against disasters that might destroy the files.

Ans backup

8.7.3.9 _____ usually consists of the destruction of an organization's website, often in an attempt to cause loss of confidence on the part of its customers.

Ans: Sabotage

9.5 Chapter 9 Questions

9.5.1 True-False

9.5.1.1 Memory management and hardware control are just two examples of tasks that both kinds of operating systems must deal with.

Ans: T

9.5.1.3 In a bus network, it is quite possible that two of the nodes might attempt to initiate transmission simultaneously. This is usually not a problem, since most communication media will support simultaneous communication.

Ans: F   Most communication media do not support simultaneous communication.

9.5.1.5 Some of the tasks of a network OS are similar to those of any OS for an individual computer.

Ans: T

9.5.1.7 The more authorization privileges a user receives, the stronger the authentication should be

Ans: T

9.5.2 Multiple Choice

9.5.2.1 Individual computers run client operating systems, while network systems create the software infrastructure necessary for _____ networks to function
   a. wireless
   b. local
   c. wide area
   d. all of the above
   e. none of the above

9.5.2.3 To use the _____ network topology, it must be supported/implemented by the operating systems on each of the nodes in the network
a. bus
b. ring
c. star
d. all of the above
e. none of the above

9.5.2.5 In a _____ topology each node is connected to two other nodes
a. bus
b. ring
c. star
d. all of the above
e. none of the above

9.5.2.7 _____ is an example peer to peer operating system
a. AppleShare
b. LANTastic
c. Windows for Workgroups
d. all of the above
e. none of the above

9.5.3 Completion

9.5.3.1 A computer network is a collection of computing devices interconnected by some communication medium.
- These devices are often referred to as _____ of the network.

Ans: nodes

9.5.3.3 On bus networks operating systems must use a media _____ control technology, such as CSMA/CD

Ans: access

9.5.3.5 In a(n) _____ topology information transmission is subject to some delay, since a message will be retransmitted several times before it reaches its intended target

Ans: ring

9.5.3.7 _____ responsibilities require network managers to track the services that users are accessing as well as the amount of network resources they are consuming

Ans: Accounting

10.9 Chapter 10 Questions

10.9.1 True-False

10.9.1.1 Files are collections of information stored on disk or other nonvolatile medium.

Ans: T

10.9.1.3 A record must be of fixed length

Ans: F A record may be of fixed length or variable length

10.9.1.5 In some sophisticated systems, access controls can be applied at the record, or even the field level

Ans: T

10.9.1.7 There are several different ways that a programmer might choose to organize his files

Ans: T

10.9.1.9 Sequential file structure does not perform well with applications that do frequent searches

Ans: T

10.9.1.11 Although they support quick efficient access to information, multiple index files introduce extra complications (and time) in insertion/deletion operations

Ans: T

10.9.1.13 A number of techniques have been used to keep track of disk space available for allocation.

Ans: T

10.9.2 Multiple Choice

10.9.2.1 In order for a file system to provide the desired functionality, files should: _____
   a.   Have a (reasonably) long term existence
   b.   Contain information/data in a form that makes it reasonably accessible.
   c.   Be protected from access by unauthorized users/processes
   d.   all of the above
   e.   none of the above

10.9.2.3 _____ is/are responsible for starting I/O operations on the physical device
   a.   Device Drivers
   b.   Basic file system
   c.   Basic I/O supervisor
   d.   Logical I/O
   e.   none of the above

10.9.2.5 _____ select(s) the device on which I/O is to be performed
   a.   Device Drivers
   b.   Basic file system
   c.   Basic I/O supervisor
   d.   Logical I/O
   e.   none of the above

10.9.2.7 The _____ is the most common form of file structure
  a. pile
  b. sequential file
  c. indexed sequential file
  d. indexed file
  e. none of the above

10.9.2.9 With the hashed file structure,
  a. data access is efficient and insertion/deletion operations can be carried out very quickly
  b.   insertion/deletion operations can be carried out very quickly, although data access can be inefficient
  c. data access is efficient but insertion/deletion operations can be a little slow
  d. data access can be inefficient and insertion/deletion operations are somewhat slow
  e. none of the above

10.9.2.11 The _____ blocking system avoids wasted storage space but is difficult to implement
  a. fixed length
  b. fixed length unspanned
  c. variable length spanned
  d. variable length unspanned
  e. none of the above

10.9.2.13 _____ allocation is the most popular form of allocation
  a. contiguous
  b. chained
  c. indexed
  d. all of the above are about equally popular
  e. none of the above

10.9.3 Completion

10.9.3.1 For most users, the _____ system is one of the most important parts of an operating system

Ans: file

10.9.3.3 A(n) _____ is a collection of related fields that would be treated as a unit

Ans: record

10.9.3.5 Although the addition of an index improves the efficiency of the search operations in an ISAM file, it does nothing for the problems involved with insertion/deletion operations. This problem is addressed by the addition of a(n) "_____ file"

Ans: overflow

Endnotes:

i   Images of microprocessors appearing on Wikipedia
produced by Christian Bassow and Peter1912,
released into public domain and released for use as long as licensing requirements are
followed.

ii   Generic Figure of a **Dual Core CPU** Originally created by **Dennis Schmitz**, 18 Dec 2004
(UTC); converted to SVG by **CountingPine**, 8 June 2007
This work has been released into the **public domain** by its author, **Dennis Schmitz at
English Wikipedia**

iii   From "*Computer Organization and Architecture*", by William Stallings, Pearson

iv   Kernel Layout
From Wikimedia Commons, the free media repository
Author Bobbo
file is licensed under the **Creative Commons Attribution-Share Alike 3.0 Unported** license.

v   Overviews of monolithic and microkernel architectures
From Wikimedia Commons, the free media repository
Author (Mattia Gentilini) has released images into public domain

vi   From "*Computer Organization and Architecture*", by William Stallings, Pearson

vii   From "*Computer Organization and Architecture*", by William Stallings, Pearson

viii   https://stackoverflow.com/questions/34512/what-is-a-deadlock

ix   From "*Computer Organization and Architecture*", by William Stallings, Pearson

x   From "*Computer Organization and Architecture*", by William Stallings, Pearson

xi   http://www.sci.brooklyn.cuny.edu/~jniu/teaching/csc33200/files/0924-
ProcessConceptAndState.pdf

xii   http://www.sci.brooklyn.cuny.edu/~jniu/teaching/csc33200/files/0924-
ProcessConceptAndState.pdf

xiii   http://www.sci.brooklyn.cuny.edu/~jniu/teaching/csc33200/files/0924-
ProcessConceptAndState.pdf

xiv   https://www.tutorialspoint.com/operating_system/os_io_hardware.htm

xv   Neetu Goel, R.B. Garg| A Comparative Study of CPU Scheduling Algorithms
International Journal of Graphics & Image Processing |Vol 2|issue 4|November 2012

xvi   Simplified Structure of the Linux Kernel
Simplified illustration of the structure of the **Linux kernel**; based on page 851 in *Modern
Operating Systems* (ISBN 013359162X) by Andrew Stuart Tanenbaum.
This image is licensed under the **Creative Commons Attribution-Share Alike 4.0 International**
license

xvii   https://www.cs.uic.edu/~jbell/CourseNotes/OperatingSystems/5_CPU_Scheduling.html

xviii   https://www.cs.uic.edu/~jbell/CourseNotes/OperatingSystems/5_CPU_Scheduling.html

xix   www.cs.uic.edu/~jbell/CourseNotes/OperatingSystems/5_CPU_Scheduling.html

xx   From "*Computer Organization and Architecture*", by William Stallings, Pearson

xxi   From "*Computer Organization and Architecture*", by William Stallings, Pearson

xxii   Cache,associative-fill-both.png
From Wikimedia Commons, the free media repository
This file is licensed under the **Creative Commons Attribution-Share Alike 3.0 Unported**
license. Subject to **disclaimers**.

[xxiii] Heron2/MistWiz - modified version of Disk-structure.svg by MistWiz
Author has released image into public domain

[xxiv] From "*Computer Organization and Architecture*", by William Stallings, Pearson

[xxv] By en:User:Cburnett - Own work., Permission is granted to copy, distribute and/or modify this document under the terms of the GNU Free Documentation License,

[xxvi] By en:User:Cburnett - Own work., Permission is granted to copy, distribute and/or modify this document under the terms of the GNU Free Documentation License,

[xxvii] Author knakts, Permission is granted to copy, distribute and/or modify this document under the terms of the GNU Free Documentation License,

[xxviii] By en:User:Cburnett - Own work., Permission is granted to copy, distribute and/or modify this document under the terms of the GNU Free Documentation License,

[xxix] By en:User:Cburnett - Own work., Permission is granted to copy, distribute and/or modify this document under the terms of the GNU Free Documentation License

[xxx] By en:User:Cburnett - Own work., Permission is granted to copy, distribute and/or modify this document under the terms of the GNU Free Documentation License

[xxxi] By en:User:Cburnett - Own work., Permission is granted to copy, distribute and/or modify this document under the terms of the GNU Free Documentation License

[xxxii] This work has been released into the public domain by its author, GW_Simulations

[xxxiii] This work has been released into the public domain by its author, GW_Simulations.

[xxxiv] This work has been released into the public domain by its author, GW_Simulations

[xxxv] Image from Operating Systems: Internals and Design Principles, 7'th edition, by William Stallings

[xxxvi] Images from Operating Systems: Internals and Design Principles, 7'th edition, by William Stallings

[xxxvii] Image from Operating Systems: Internals and Design Principles, 7'th edition, by William Stallings

[xxxviii] Image from Operating Systems: Internals and Design Principles, 7'th edition, by William Stallings

[xxxix] Image from Operating Systems: Internals and Design Principles, 7'th edition, by William Stallings

[xl] Image from Operating Systems: Internals and Design Principles, 7'th edition, by William Stallings

[xli] Image from Operating Systems: Internals and Design Principles, 7'th edition, by William Stallings